FOOD FOR SPORT

Nathan J. Smith, M.D.
University of Washington

BULL PUBLISHING COMPANY

P.O. Box 208
Palo Alto, California 94302

BERKELEY SERIES IN NUTRITION

Food for Sport, Nathan J. Smith, M.D. (1976)

The Berkeley Series in Nutrition is a series of significant books about foods and nutrition, as they relate to the health and well being of people. It is our intent that all publications in this series will be carefully reviewed and evaluated before publication, to insure that the information is consistent with the current understanding of scientific research studies and practices in nutrition as it relates to the needs of humans.

Some books will provide an overview of the subject for the reader wanting reliable non-technical information. Others will be useful as college text books in non-major and majors courses in nutrition. Still other books in the series are expected to contain specialized, technical information, for the professional in food and nutrition and related fields.

George M. Briggs, Ph.D.
Professor of Nutrition
Biochemist, Agriculture Experiment Station
University of California, Berkeley

Helen D. Ullrich, M.A., R.D.
Editor, Journal of NUTRITION EDUCATION
Lecturer in Nutrition
University of California, Berkeley
Editors

Cover: *UPI photo of Olga Korbut*
Design: *Jill Casty*

ISBN 0-915950-03-0—paperback
ISBN 0-915950-04-9—hardbound

Library of Congress
catalog no. 76-4092

INTRODUCTION

Since the days of "a good 5-cent cigar" this old world has needed a readable book on nutrition, and Dr. Smith's *Food for Sport* fills this need. It has a lot of information for athletes, coaches, doctors, and trainers; but it will be of equal benefit to the non-athlete and sometimes athlete, to the big meat and potato eater, to the vegetarian, to the underweight, and to those who wish they were.

Food for Sport is pleasantly readable, with enough anecdotal material to make the important facts memorable. The chapters are organized according to topics of popular interest, each with a summary. His "suggestions for non-meat eaters" should be on every college bulletin board, and the book itself should be in the hands of every athlete, from grade school jumpropers to international Olympians.

I predict it will be translated into many languages and read throughout the world.

Daniel F. Hanley, M.D.
Chairman, Medical & Training
    Services Committee
United States Olympic Committee

Member, Medical Commission
International Olympic Committee

*Dedicated with sincere respect
to the athletes of Franklin High.*

Contents

FOREWORD

one _____1

NUTRIENTS: THE BASIC BUILDING BLOCKS
What They Are, What They Do, Where They Are Found

Water / Minerals / Vitamins (fat-soluble and water-soluble vitamins, vitamin functions) / Fats (The composition and sources of dietary fat) / Carbohydrates (carbohydrates as an energy source, foods that provide carbohydrates for energy) / Proteins (sources and composition of protein, protein requirements for the athlete) / Some principal nutrients

two _____23

THE BASIC DIET
The Starting Point

The importance of a varied diet / Nutritional requirements for healthy individuals / The Four Food Group plan / Milk and milk products / Meat and high protein foods / Vegetables and fruits / Cereals and grains / The Basic Diet

three _____35

**NONTRADITIONAL DIETS
AND DIETARY SUPPLEMENTS**
Are They Adequate For An Athlete?

Vegetarian and other meatless diets / A lacto-vegetarian diet / Non-conventional (Zen macrobiotic, fruitarian) diets / Organic foods / Weight control diets / Vitamin supplements (Vitamins E and C) / Protein supplements

four _____ 51

GAINING OR LOSING WEIGHT
Calories And The Art Of Controlling Them

How energy is measured / The body's use of energy / Man's energy expenditure / Energy expenditure in various sports / The energy contribution of various foods / Altering energy balance / Gaining weight / A 6000-Calorie weight gain diet / Promoting weight gain with androgen hormones / Losing weight / Who should lose weight? / Planning a weight reduction program / A 2000-Calorie reducing diet

five _____ 73

THE ENERGY DEMANDS OF THE ATHLETE
The Power—Where It Comes From, And How To Maximize it

The sources of energy / The ATP-PC system / Glycogen / Fats and carbohydrates / The importance of training and diet / Diet management for all-out effort of short duration / Meeting the energy needs for intermediate length events (The High Performance Diet) / Dietary considerations for endurance contests / Liquid meals

six _____ 89

THE ATHLETE'S NEED FOR WATER AND SALT
What You Can Do About Fluid Balance

The importance of adequate hydration / The distribution and regulation of body water / The water requirements of the athlete / The athlete's need for salt / The critical role of water in the prevention of heat disorders

seven _____ 105

IRON NUTRITION
The Need For Iron

Iron metabolism / Iron needs / Iron in the diet / Individuals in particular risk of iron deficiency / Sources of iron / The prevention of iron deficiency

eight _____115

THE PRE-GAME MEAL
AND EATING DURING COMPETITION
Tips For Preparation At Home And Away

Important factors in pre-game eating / The goals of the pre-game diet / Food intake before competition / The liquid pre-game meal / Meeting the needs of energy and hydration during competition / Feeding the traveling team / Low-cost pre-event meals

nine _____127

WRESTLING AND OTHER
WEIGHT CONTROL SPORTS
A Sound Weight Control Program

The effects of inadequate weight programs / The High Performance Diet / The ideal competing weight / The essentials of a weight control program / The nutritional demands of growth / Other weight control sports / Diuretics and cathartics

ten _____143

NUTRITION FOR THE
ELEMENTARY SCHOOL ATHLETE
The Needs Of The Young Competitor

The beginnings of good health habits / Diet recommendations for the elementary school athlete / Nutritional abuses of the young athlete

eleven _____151

FITNESS FOR THE OLDER ATHLETE
Keeping In Shape During The Later Years

The decline of fitness / A diet for adult fitness / Cholesterol in the diet / Alcohol in the adult's diet / Decreasing energy needs of the older adult / Physical activity / The diet for the serious adult competitor

A WORD ABOUT SOME SPECIFIC SPORTS
Summaries Of The Most Important Factors

Basketball / Swimming / Crew / Tennis / Gymnastics and Figure Skating / Football / Track and Field, Cross Country / Wrestling / Hiking, Mountaineering, Cross-Country Skiing / Other Sports (Soccer, Ice Hockey, Bicycle Racing, Ice Skating)

APPENDIX A
U.S. Recommended Daily Allowances

APPENDIX B
Alternate Basic Diet Menus

APPENDIX C
Weight-Loss Graphs

APPENDIX D
Information On Skin-Fold Measurements

APPENDIX E
Statement On Heat Injuries And Distance Running

APPENDIX F
Participation By Girls/Oarswomen

FOREWORD

This book is written for "the athlete"—of any age, male or female, casual participant, intense amateur, or accomplished professional. For what is written here has come out of the privilege of listening to the nutrition-related problems described by these people over the past several years, and with their help and interest seeking out solutions—for both improved performance and better health.

It has become increasingly clear in recent years that knowledge of nutrition and exercise physiology have reached a level where certain dietary recommendations can be made specifically, for particular needs of particular athletes. Where possible, such recommendations have been made here. In addition, our experience with the intensely competitive athlete has shown that he or she often pursues (with enthusiasm) nutrition-related practices which are ineffective, counterproductive, or even dangerous. They are identified and discussed here.

This book is about food—what it is, what it does, and how it can be chosen selectively to maximize physical performance. As indicated, it is directed to a wide range of readers: the casual sports participant, who would like to learn more about the essentials of good eating; the student of nutrition, exploring the basic principles of food and energy; the highly skilled athlete, hoping to perform as effectively as possible; and the coach, trainer, or parent, seeking dietary advice for the team. It is really a book for all active people. A good diet cannot, in itself, give them fitness or championship medals, but a poor diet can ruin their chances of either.

It has been my hope in writing this book that participants in all sports will find information here that will enhance their understanding of the nutritional needs for their various sports—so they can achieve a better level of athletic performance .·. . and of lifelong health.

Even this modest effort would never have seen the light of day without a most understanding wife, and a prodding and helpful publisher. To both Marcy, my wife, and David Bull, the publisher, my sincere thanks and deep appreciation.

NATHAN J. SMITH, M.D.
Seattle, Washington
January 1976

FOOD FOR SPORT

This book has been written by a physician who is an authority in both nutrition and athletics. The book is for athletes of either sex and all ages, from the pre-school baseball player to the grandparent jogger. Whether you enjoy athletics as a hobby or a profession, this book can help you.

Dr. Smith has been the physician for athletic teams and a researcher in a field related to nutrition. He has lectured and written extensively on problems of anemias in children. He writes this book from scientific knowledge and practical experience.

The book has been extensively reviewed by nutritionists and physical education specialists. As a result it reflects the consensus of opinion about sound practices in nutrition as they relate to exercise. Its easily understood, non-technical approach will provide useful information for the coach, trainer, parent, athlete, and casual sportsman wanting to know how diet can help achieve athletic results, as well as life-long health.

Editors, Berkeley Series in Nutrition

one

NUTRIENTS: THE BASIC BUILDING BLOCKS

Athletes make special demands of their bodies, and must be physically prepared to meet those demands. The starting point is sound nutritional knowledge and practice. Yet dedicated competitors, who will sacrifice so much to excel, often ruin their chances with inefficient, sometimes harmful diets. Reduced stamina and strength take their toll, and the effects on performance are clear.

With some basic knowledge of food, and how it supplies the body's needs, it is usually a simple matter to reverse the situation; the athlete who has competed at a disadvantage can in fact become the one with the advantage.

FOODS AND NUTRIENTS

Long before we are old enough to develop taste preferences, food is meeting our nutritional needs. It comes to us through the umbilical lifeline, already affecting our growth and development. We later find our food lined in garden rows, stacked on supermarket shelves, tucked in kitchen ovens, primped on restaurant platters, popped from drive-in windows, and locked in hallway vending machines. Food is found in many places and in many guises. And beyond satisfying the biochemical and energy needs of our bodies, this variety gives us eating pleasure, both culinary and social.

Most of our social functions, in fact, are associated with food: the dinner party, the business luncheon, the wedding feast, the holiday banquet, and so forth. Lovers identify certain foods with particularly tender meanings, while the grandstand hot dog has a universal association of its own. Since man first picked up a root to share it, food has become a form of communication, and has always been more than something to eat.

In physiological terms, food satisfies three fundamental body needs: (1) the need for energy, (2) the need for new tissue and tissue repair, and (3) the need for chemical regulators of the metabolic functions constantly taking place in the body. These three needs are provided for by specific components of food called "nutrients." There are six classes of nutrients, each with very precise chemical characteristics and each suited to meet very specific body needs. The six classes are: water, minerals, vitamins, proteins, fats, and carbohydrates.

Water

Water is the most "essential"[1] of all nutrients inasmuch as it takes priority over all others in the need for a constant and uninterrupted supply. It is of particular concern to the athlete. An adequate supply of water is necessary for all energy production in the body, for temperature control, particularly during periods of vigorous exercise, and for the expeditious elimination of the by-products of cell metabolism. Depriving the body of water strikingly limits energy and endurance. Because water is abundantly available and essentially free of cost, it is easily overlooked by the athlete as a critical element for optimal performance. (See Chapter 6 for greater detail.)

Minerals

Mineral nutrients are considered in two groups: those present in relatively large amounts in the body and those needed in very small amounts (the "trace" minerals). The first group—all available in the foods we eat—are sodium, potassium, calcium, phosphorus, magnesium, sulfur, and various chlorides.

[1]"Essential" nutrients are those the body cannot synthesize. They must, therefore, be provided by food intake.

Sodium and potassium are highly water-soluble metallic ions, widely distributed throughout nature and in abundant supply in all foods. Sodium is found primarily in body fluids in the fluid spaces between body cells (the extracellular fluids). It is the chief metallic ion in body sweat, and a significant amount may be lost in profuse and protracted sweating. Under any but the most extreme circumstances, however, the sodium lost in sweat and other body excretions will be readily replaced through the sodium content of the normal diet. In fact, given the usual abundance of salt in the American diet, the concern should be for too much, not too little. (See Chapter 6.)

Potassium is the principal metallic ion within body cells. It plays an essential role in the function of muscle cells, and a deficit of potassium is associated with muscular weakness and fatigue. Fruit juices, bananas, apricots, soybeans, and potatoes are excellent sources of potassium. Along with sodium, it determines the amount of water held in the tissues. This is an important factor in athletic performance and will be more fully discussed in Chapter 6.

Calcium, phosphorus, and magnesium are present in the body in relatively large amounts, principally bound to protein molecules as structural units in bone. Milk and milk products are the main sources of calcium and phosphorus in the American diet. In the absence of milk, a variety of plant foods, such as broccoli, spinach, and other leafy greens, can provide calcium. Phosphorus and magnesium needs can be met by whole wheat cereals, red meats, and certain vegetables, such as kidney beans and lentils. On the whole, calcium, phosphorus, and magnesium deficiency disorders are not found in this country.

There are at least 14 trace minerals that must be ingested by humans for the maintenance of health. Although the amounts required are relatively small, the need for these minerals is very real. Iron, iodine, and fluorine are trace minerals of particular concern. Fluorine is essential for healthy dental and bone formation. In many parts of the United States, the concentration in water is very low, and adding fluorides to community water supplies has greatly improved dental health by reducing dental caries.

Iodine is an essential component of thyroxin, the hormone produced by the thyroid gland. It is obtained primarily from water supplies; and in certain areas in the United States, the level of iodine concentration in the water is very low. These areas once had widespread iodine deficiency problems, often causing an enlargement of the thyroid gland known as "goiter," but because of the general use of iodized salt in the American diet, iodine should no longer be a problem.

Zinc is a trace mineral which many nutritionists believe should be a matter of greater concern. It is required for normal growth, tissue repair, blood cell formation, and reproductive function, and may not be present in adequate amounts in the small diets of inactive people. Whole grains, and most meats are the principal sources of zinc in the diet. Only future knowledge will determine whether dietary supplementation of zinc is necessary.

Iron is the trace mineral present in largest amounts in the body. It is an essential component in the energy metabolism of every body cell and is highly concentrated in the red pigment of muscles and blood. For a variety of reasons the dietary intake of iron is frequently inadequate to meet body needs. Since iron deficiency compromises energy production and reduces endurance, assuring an adequate intake of iron is of great importance to the athlete. Iron-rich foods—such as meats, meat substitutes, leafy vegetables, dates and raisins—should be a regular part of any diet. Since iron deserves particular attention, Chapter 7 is devoted entirely to the subject.

Vitamins

Vitamins are organic substances which function as chemical regulators and are necessary for growth and the maintenance of life. Because they are needed in such small amounts, they were the last "essential" nutrients to be discovered. Contrary to popular belief, the foods ordinarily consumed by active individuals from a varied diet contain a sufficient supply of vitamins to meet body needs. In fact some of them are required in such small amounts (vitamin E, pantothenic acid and biotin), that even the most irregular and poorly selected diets provide sufficient amounts.

Vitamin deficiencies did not become apparent until the advent of the industrial revolution, urbanization, and sea travel, when mankind moved away from the farm and a varied diet of recently harvested foodstuffs. Scurvy (from insufficient vitamin C) developed in sailors who spent long weeks at sea; the impoverished people of Southeast Asia, who restricted their diets to polished rice, were found to have vitamin B deficiencies; and rickets made its appearance in infants when crowded slums appeared in European cities, often depriving their inhabitants of sufficient contact with the vitamin D-producing rays of the sun.

Fat-Soluble and Water-Soluble Vitamins. The 14 known vitamins are divided into two groups: those soluble in fat and those soluble in water. Vitamins A, D, E, and K are soluble in fat; vitamin C and the B-complex vitamins are soluble in water. The solubility characteristic is important in determining whether the body can store the vitamin or whether the supply must be constantly replenished. It also determines a vitamin's toxic potential when taken in excess of body needs.

Vitamin C and the B-complex vitamins are soluble in water and thus are not stored to any significant degree in the body; therefore, the diet must constantly replenish the supplies. The daily requirement for vitamin C can be met with the natural sources of leafy vegetables, most raw vegetables, and citrus fruits. Sources for the B vitamins are listed in the accompanying table. If one does not get enough of the water-soluble vitamins, clinical evidence of a deficiency state will develop after a few weeks. When intake is greater than body needs, the excess is excreted in the urine.

Excess fat-soluble vitamins (A, D, E, and K) are stored in the liver and, to a lesser extent, in the fatty tissues of the body. If stores have accumulated during a period of excess, an individual may get along on an inadequate intake of a fat-soluble vitamin for many months, even years.

Vitamins are widely distributed in the foods that make up the typical American diet and, as a rule, are eaten in proportion to the total caloric intake. Therefore, people eating the generous amounts called for in times of growth and active exercise will be receiving an adequate supply of nearly all the vitamins. Vitamin C and folic acid (a member of the vitamin B group) are exceptions. The foods in which they are found in highest concentration are foods which make minimal contributions to caloric intake. In order to provide these vitamins, an uncooked or lightly steamed vegetable or some fresh fruit should be included in the daily diet.

Vitamin Functions.   It is important for the athlete to recognize the general functions of vitamins in the body; i.e., what vitamins do, and particularly what they do not do. Vitamins function primarily as regulators, governing the hundreds of biochemical reactions involved in organ function, growth, and energy metabolism. *They do not contribute significantly to body structure nor are they a direct source of body energy.* Thus, the vitamin needs of an active athlete are generally no greater than those of the most sedentary individual—and the unfortunate tendency toward taking excess vitamin supplements for athletic performance is a matter of particular concern. (See Chapter 3 for more on this subject.)

One B vitamin, thiamine, is an exception, since it is required in proportion to carbohydrate intake (and very active athletes as a group may be expected to eat more carbohydrate). Fortunately thiamine is also present in primary carbohydrate sources, such as breads and other foods made with whole-grain or fortified grain products. It is thus abundant in the typical American diet.

No one food contains sufficient levels of all the vitamins needed by man, but a varied diet selection from different groups of food provides an adequate supply and eliminates any need for medicinal vitamin supplements. After infancy

VITAMINS: DIETARY SOURCES AND PRINCIPAL FUNCTIONS

Fat-soluble Vitamins

VITAMINS	SOURCES	FUNCTIONS	DEFICIENCY STATES
Vitamin A (Provitamin A)	Liver, egg yolk, milk, butter (Vitamin A) Yellow vegetables, greens (Provitamin A)	Adaptation to dim light Resistance to infection Prevents eye and skin disorders	Night blindness Xerophthalmia (softening of eye structures—blindness)
Vitamin D	Sunlight, fish, eggs, fortified dairy products	Facilitates absorption of calcium	Rickets
Vitamin E	Vegetable oils, greens	Prevents oxidation of essential vitamins and fatty acids	
Vitamin K	Greens, liver	Blood clotting	Hemorrhage disease

Water-soluble Vitamins

VITAMINS	SOURCES	FUNCTIONS	DEFICIENCY STATES
Thiamine (B_1)	Meat, whole grain cereals, milk, legumes	Energy metabolism Formation of niacin	Beriberi
Riboflavin (B_2)	Milk, fish, eggs, meat, green vegetables	Energy metabolism	Mouth and lip lesions and loss of vision
Niacin	Peanut butter, whole grain cereals, greens, meat, poultry, fish	Energy metabolism Fatty acid synthesis	Limitation of energy production Pellagra

VITAMINS	SOURCES	FUNCTIONS	DEFICIENCY STATES
Pyridoxine (B$_6$)	Whole grain cereals, bananas, meats, spinach, cabbage, lima beans	Protein metabolism Hemoglobin synthesis Production of energy from glycogen	Convulsions Anemia
Folic Acid (Folacin)	Greens, mushrooms, liver	Blood cell production, growth	Anemia
Cobalamin (B$_{12}$)	Animal foods	Blood cell production Energy metabolism Central nervous system function	Pernicious anemia, neuro-muscular weakness
Ascorbic Acid (Vitamin C)	Citrus fruits, tomatoes, strawberries, potatoes, papaya, broccoli, cabbage	Formation of supporting tissues particularly in capillaries Metabolism of vitamins; i.e., folic acid	Scurvy
Pantothenic Acid	Whole grain cereals, organ meats	Hemoglobin formation Fat metabolism	No deficiency states have been clinically identified for Biotin and Pantothenic Acid. They are required in such small amounts that they are not a consideration in diet planning.
Biotin	Cereal, nuts, legumes, meats, egg yolk, milk	Carbohydrate energy metabolism Fat and protein metabolism	

vitamin supplements are needed only by those with very specific disease-related health problems, or by those who, for any reason, have been deprived of an adequate diet for a prolonged period of time.

Vitamins and minerals do not contribute significantly to the bulk of the diet. It is mainly composed of water and the remaining three classes of nutrients: fats, carbohydrates, and proteins. These provide the body's energy and contribute the structural components for growth and tissue repair.

Fats

Fats are essential in our diet. They are greasy substances, not soluble in water but in a variety of organic solvents such as ether and benzene. Fats are the most concentrated source of food energy, containing twice as many calories per unit of weight as either protein or carbohydrate. They are, therefore, uniquely well suited for storage of excess energy.

In addition, fats are the only source of linoleic acid, an essential nutrient which the human body cannot synthesize from other food sources. It is needed for growth and for the maintenance of healthy skin. Fats also provide the necessary vehicle for fat-soluble vitamins, and a diet too low in fat could be deficient in certain of the fat-soluble vitamins.

Fat adds palatability to our food, and is often abundant in foods desired for flavor; as a result, it is easy to get an excess. The well-marbled steak, the whipped cream on the strawberry shortcake, the lemon butter brushed over the broiled salmon, and the sour cream on the baked potato are all foods high in fat. They are eaten because "they taste good." But fat is not only flavorful, it also has a high satiety value. Some of the feeling of satisfaction and fullness after a fine dinner is due to the fact that fatty foods leave the stomach slowly—an important concern in planning pre-game meals for the athlete.

The Composition and Sources of Dietary Fat.　Such terms as "saturated" and "polyunsaturated," "triglyceride," and "cholesterol" are appearing with increasing frequency on supermarket labels and in our everyday conversation. They relate to the fats in our diets, and anyone interested in fitness should understand their meaning.

The structural units of fats are fatty acids. Depending on their chemical structure, they will be either solid (saturated fat), such as those present in relatively high amounts in most animal fats; or they will be liquid (unsaturated fat), such as the major fatty acids present in oils of vegetable and fish origin. Most populations which eat large quantities of animal fats, in the form of meat, eggs, and dairy products, have a high incidence of atherosclerosis and cardiovascular disease. The American population provides an excellent example, and the American Heart Association has strongly recommended that we reduce the amounts of saturated fat in our diet.

Fats may be "visible," as when surrounding an expensive steak, or dressing a salad with oil. Other forms of dietary fat may not be so apparent, but nonetheless contribute significantly to fat intake: in the marbling of the steak between the meat fibers, the olive in the martini, the avocado slices on the salad, the chocolate in the dessert, and the margarine or butter used in an unending variety of foods. The ceremonial steak dinner at the football training table, the patio party, and the expense-account dinner are all meals high in fat, much of it saturated fat of animal origin. Overenthusiasm for such diets is thought by some authorities to represent a significant threat to present and future health.[2]

The typical American diet provides approximately 45 per cent of its calories in the form of fat. (This compares with the typical Southeast Asian diet, which generally contains less than 10 per cent, and with certain northwest Indians and Eskimos who often receive as much as 60 per cent.) At the beginning of this century, only 25 per cent of the calories

---

[2]There are nutritionists who claim that the plea for diets low in animal fats does not take into account the wide metabolic variations among different people. For those individuals with high levels, there are other diets which may be more appropriate. It should be noted, therefore, that the diets in this book are offered as prudent diets for the general population, which may be followed with a good bit of flexibility

in the American diet came from fat. As we grew more affluent, the expensive and flavorful fatty foods grew in popularity, our physical activity decreased, and there was a marked increase in the incidence of degenerative vascular disease.

In the light of present knowledge, it would appear wise to reduce the caloric contribution of fats in the American diet, particularly the diet of the young male athlete—to between 30 and 35 per cent, and to make sure that half of that fat be unsaturated, of vegetable or fish origin. (This has been recommended as a prudent diet for the average American male by the American Heart Association.)

Carbohydrates

The most efficient (and generally the most inexpensive) sources of food energy are the various sugars and starches which comprise the group known as "carbohydrates." These are provided through plants, which make available energy from the sun. Taking carbon from carbon dioxide in the air, along with hydrogen and oxygen from water in the soil, plants capture the sun's energy and synthesize it into sugars and starches of varying complexity. Each is made up of basic carbon, oxygen, and hydrogen units.

The basic structural unit of all carbohydrates is the simple sugar, "glucose." During digestion and metabolism all carbohydrates are eventually broken down and converted to this simple compound for use as the body's principal source of energy. In the discussion of the body's energy system (Chapter 5), the importance of glucose will be evident. "Sucrose," or table sugar, and the starch in cereal and grain products, are combinations of simple sugars which the body uses either immediately or after conversion to glucose. The sugars in honey, fruits, and milk are all converted to glucose by the liver, following their absorption from the gastrointestinal tract.

The milk sugar, "lactose," is broken down into simple sugars by the enzyme "lactase" located in the cells lining the intestinal tract. In most of the people of the world, with the exception of northern European and North American white populations, this intestinal enzyme becomes progressively less active after three or four years of age. As a result, they lose their ability to efficiently digest large amounts of milk sugar and will avoid the intake of large quantities of milk and dairy products. Undigested milk sugar remaining in the bowel will cause cramping, mild diarrhea, and general discomfort. Most, but not all, American Blacks and Indians cannot tolerate more than one or two glasses of milk at a time, and milk and dairy products will not be a prominent part of their diet. But many "unprocessed" cheeses and high-quality yogurts have had their milk sugar digested by bacterial action, and can be eaten comfortably by those unable to digest milk sugar.

Carbohydrates As An Energy Source.   As we stated earlier, the sugar in carbohydrate food provides the most efficient and readily available source of energy. Fats are a more concentrated energy source, appropriate for long-term storage of energy. But the conversion process involved in energy utilization is more complicated, and consequently the energy is not so readily available. (Protein is the least efficient energy source. Its component amino acids must be converted to carbohydrate and go through additional reactions before they can be utilized for energy; and the by-products of this metabolism must be excreted by the kidneys.)

The simple sugars from digested carbohydrates are absorbed from the intestinal tract and taken via the bloodstream to the liver, where they are converted to glucose. Much of this glucose then reenters the bloodstream and is transported to body tissues, principally the brain and muscles. A relatively small amount is converted to "glycogen," a form of carbohydrate which is readily stored in either the muscles or liver. (The importance of glycogen storage, as an important source of energy in athletic performance, is discussed in Chapter 5.)

In addition to supplying the muscles and brain, glucose must be constantly transported to other vital organs, such as the heart and kidneys. The constant glucose supply, particularly to the brain, is essential for an optimum sense of awareness and for the quick reflexes necessary for top athletic performance. An inadequate supply of glucose, particularly to the central nervous system, results in feelings of weakness, hunger, nausea, and dizziness.

It is important to note that this primary source of energy, carbohydrate, cannot be stored in significant amounts by the body. An average well-nourished man has only enough glucose and glycogen in his bloodstream and tissues to meet his energy demands for about half a day of sedentary activity. This should come as no surprise to the student who has missed breakfast and lunch and can recall the symptoms of glucose depletion he felt by late afternoon. He probably felt hungry, unable to concentrate and lethargic. Since the body cannot store significant amounts, it is obvious that an active person should take some form of carbohydrate at regular intervals throughout the day. A very large, active athlete may function best with occasional high carbohydrate snacks in addition to the carbohydrate contribution from the regular daily meals.

The University basketball coaches recently sent a freshman player to our Sports Medicine Nutrition Clinic because his afternoon practice performance had been deteriorating. He was found to be in good health and his eating habits were not unusual. He was living in a dormitory, where he regularly ate a large breakfast before going to class at 8:30 and a generous lunch three hours later when the dining room first opened at 11:30. He would have nothing more to eat until the evening dinner hour.

It was apparent that he was exhausting his energy stores midway through the afternoon practice session, and was lacking endurance and unable to concentrate. He was advised to eat a sizable high carbohydrate snack just before the dining room closed at 2:00 p.m. The new diet schedule with the added midday intake allowed him to maintain a sense of well-being throughout the afternoon practice sessions. His performance improved and he played varsity basketball during his freshman year.

Foods That Provide Carbohydrate for Energy. There is very little glucose, as such, in the daily diet. However, more complex sugars, which the body converts to glucose, have become increasingly prominent in the American diet. For example, Americans now eat more than one hundred pounds of common table sugar, or "sucrose," each year.[3] The primary sources of sucrose are sugar cane and sugar beets. Most of the products made from these sources are relatively expensive, and they are widely used only in the affluent societies of the industrialized nations.

Less expensive but still readily available sources of carbohydrates come from the starches contained in the inner portion of cereal grains such as wheat, rice, and corn. Following harvesting, the seed grain is milled, and the protective coat or "bran" is removed, along with the germ or embryo of the grain seed. The protein and starch remain; and the milled product is what we know as "flour." The less-refined, unmilled grains, such as in whole wheat flours, likewise contain a full complement of grain starch.

Bread, spaghetti, pies, waffles, pancakes, doughnuts, etc. are made primarily from wheat flour and contribute wheat starch as a common source of carbohydrate. Other vegetable starches also provide significant amounts of carbohydrate. Potatoes, beans, and various kinds of tuber or root foods are dietary staples throughout the world, supplying the main sources of energy through carbohydrates. Fresh and dried fruits also contribute significant carbohydrate in the form of sugar.

Leafy vegetables, like lettuce and cabbage, and stem vegetables like celery are high in "cellulose," a large, complex carbohydrate, which represents roughage in the diet. Cellulose is generally not digested by man and therefore contributes no usable energy; but it does provide important bulk to the diet which enhances intestinal function.

Many of the dietary contributors of carbohydrates, such as bread, spaghetti, and pastry, are relatively inexpensive, and there is a popular notion that they are of low nutritional value.

[3]Sucrose is a chemical combination of glucose and fructose (which is converted to glucose in the body).

In fact they are important sources of energy and highly desirable in the diet of active sport participants. Carbohydrate from such cereal grain products, along with other sources, should contribute well over 50 per cent of the athlete's total caloric intake.

Proteins

The last of the six major classes of nutrients is protein. Throughout most of the world protein is in short supply, and there are various American myths about protein superiority as a food. Actually high-quality protein is abundantly available to most Americans and is usually eaten far in excess of body needs. Not only is the excess unnecessary, it can actually be harmful, particularly when ingested during times of intense athletic competition. The average American ingests two or three times as much protein as he needs.

To be sure, some protein is essential in our diet. It is a major structural component of all body tissue and is needed for growth and repair. In addition, it is a functional component of enzymes, hormones, antibodies, blood plasma transport mechanisms, etc. In general, proteins are inefficient sources of energy and are used for energy only when the more efficient sources, carbohydrates and fats, are not available.

Sources and Composition of Protein.   Protein is generously available in nature, both in animal tissue and in the seeds (grains) of plants. Protein from both sources is composed of the same basic structural units, amino acids. There are some 20 amino acids, linked together in an almost limitless number of combinations, each unique to a particular kind of animal or plant protein. An important chemical characteristic of amino acids is that they all contain a so-called "amino group." This nitrogen-containing amino group is converted to urea, which must be excreted in the urine, when protein is metabolized in the body. This requires water and may aggravate the dehydration of an athlete metabolizing large amounts of protein. As will be seen in Chapter 6, dehydration is often a significant problem for the athlete.

Of the entire group of amino acids, there are nine that cannot be made by man and must be provided by his diet. These are recognized as the "essential amino acids." If any one of this group is absent from the protein sources in the diet, there will be limitations on growth and body function.

It has been thought that the most efficient way to meet protein needs is to eat foods that contain essential amino acids in the same proportions as those found in the body. This theory has found support in experiments in which rats are fed protein from various sources. Milk contains the essential amino acids in proportions very similar to that of rat body protein, so it is not surprising that rats experience optimum growth when supplied with milk protein.

Feeding the rat protein of vegetable origin can also meet his protein needs, particularly if the protein comes from several sources. But because the amino acids in plant protein are generally distributed differently from those found in rat body protein, the plant proteins will be used less efficiently. Since plant proteins have lower concentrations of one or more essential amino acids than do animal proteins, they will meet the needs of human nutrition most efficiently when vegetable protein from varying sources are eaten together, so that the amino acid composition of some will complement the amino acid composition of others.

Although most Americans, and particularly active athletes, place a high priority on animal protein, one does not have to look far to find large numbers of people, even champion athletes, who are meeting their protein needs from predominantly vegetable sources. A varied diet limited to vegetables, grains, and fruits can very adequately meet human needs for protein. The needs will be met somewhat less efficiently when there is no animal protein in the diet, and larger amounts of vegetable protein will be needed. When just a small amount of animal protein is added to a predominantly vegetable diet, the additional amino acid contribution, even though modest, enhances the protein efficiency of the vegetable proteins in the diet. A large number of people take advantage of this fact by adding egg, or cheese, or other dairy

SOME PRINCIPAL NUTRIENTS: THEIR SOURCES AND FUNCTIONS

NUTRIENT	RICH SOURCES	FUNCTIONS
Protein	Meat, fish, eggs, legumes, nuts, and cereal	Growth and repair of tissue Synthesis of hormones, antibodies and enzymes Milk production during lactation Energy source (expensive and inefficient)
Fats	Oils, margarine and butter, well-larded meats, mayonnaise and salad dressing, nuts, chocolate, and peanut butter	Concentrated source of energy Efficient storage of energy Carriers of fat-soluble vitamins (A, D, E, and K) Satiety value Flavor
Carbohydrate	Cereal grain products, sugar and honey, pastries, dried fruits	Economical and efficient energy source Flavor

Important Minerals

Calcium	Dairy products, green leafy vegetables, legumes	Bone formation Enzyme reactions Blood coagulation
Iron	Liver and lean meats, soybeans, dried fruits	Hemoglobin formation Muscle growth and function Various energy-producing enzyme systems

Zinc	Shellfish, oysters, grains and meats (fruits and vegetables are poor sources)	Growth Blood cell production Tissue healing Enzyme reactions Reproductive functions
Fluorides	Water supplies, plants and animal tissues (depending on water supplies)	Formation of teeth and bones
Iodine	Fresh seafoods, water supplies in certain regions, iodized salt	Production of thyroxine
Water	All beverages, foods (vegetables and fruits), water	All bodily chemical reactions Excretory function Cooling function

products to an otherwise strictly vegetarian diet, and thus satisfy their protein needs with a so-called "lacto-ovo-vegetarian diet." See Chapter 3 for a further discussion of such diets, and a plan for lacto-vegetarian diets.

Protein Requirements of the Athlete. It is important for athletes to recognize that their athletic activity, even though it may require a high energy expenditure, will not significantly increase their need for protein. Growing young athletes have significant protein requirements, but it is in direct proportion to their needs for other essential nutrients. If they eat a varied and widely selected diet—adequate to meet their needs for energy, the essential vitamins, minerals, fatty acids, etc.—they will get all the protein they can use.

Excess protein, particularly animal protein, should be avoided. Foods such as meat, whole milk, eggs, and most cheeses may contain, in addition to their complement of high quality animal protein, an almost equal amount of saturated animal fat. Such animal protein foods tend to be expensive, and they may lead to dietary habits which are undesirable because of the accompanying high fat content. In addition, they can contribute to an immediate handicap to athletic performance because of their adverse effect on body hydration.

SUMMARY

There are six classes of nutrients: water, minerals, vitamins, carbohydrates, fats, and proteins. The so-called "essential" nutrients are those the body cannot synthesize, which must be supplied in the diet. They are: water, sources of energy (generally carbohydrates), vitamins (which by definition are essential nutrients), nine amino acid building blocks of proteins, one fatty acid, and a variety of mineral elements. To include these essential nutrients in adequate amounts requires a daily diet selected from a wide variety of foods.

The unique nutritional requirement of the athlete is his high requirement for energy. Energy is provided most efficiently by carbohydrates, to a lesser extent by fat, and least efficiently by protein.

Water, protein, fats, and minerals are the primary constituents of body tissues. Vitamins are involved in catalyzing and regulating many of the body's chemical reactions. Contrary to popular belief, athletes do not need proteins, vitamins, or minerals in exceptional amounts.

SUGGESTED READINGS AND REFERENCE WORKS

1. Deutsch, R.M.: *Realities of Nutrition.* Bull Publishing Co., Palo Alto, Calif., 1976.

2. Bogert, L.J., Briggs, G.M., and Calloway, D.H.: *Nutrition and Physical Fitness.* 9th ed., W.B. Saunders Co., Phila., Pa., 1973.

3. Deutsch, R.M.: *The Family Guide to Better Food and Better Health.* Meredith Corp., Des Moines, Iw., 1971.

4. Goodhart, R.S. and Shils, M.E.: *Modern Nutrition in Health and Disease.* 5th ed., Lea and Febiger, Philadelphia, Pa., 1973.

5. Censolazio, C.F.: "Nutrition and Athletic Performance." In: *Progressive Human Nutrition,* Vol. 1. Margens, ed. AVI Publishing Co., Westport, Conn., 1971, pp. 118-131.

two

THE
BASIC
DIET

Haphazard eating habits exact their toll eventually. At some point almost all athletes run into problems which better food choices might have prevented: insufficient stamina, difficulty concentrating, impaired strength, and unwanted weight loss (or gain), etc. And their immediate solutions are not highly specialized diets to maximize competitive performance but the sound definition of a well-balanced diet—one that will not only meet immediate needs but which will also form nutritional patterns for lifelong health.

In truth, there is no *one* diet for the athlete. Every sport makes individual energy demands that require specific dietary plans for prime performance. But there are nutritional essentials common to all such diets. This chapter discusses those essentials and how they constitute a "Basic Diet," both for the athlete, and for all of us who are generally active. Special modifications for particular athletes and specific competition will be covered in later chapters.

THE IMPORTANCE OF
A WELL-BALANCED DIET

The importance of an adequate diet was recently dramatized by the experience of a high school junior. John was an all-around performer: he was a member of the cross-country team, vice-president of the student body, and an excellent student. However, by the end of the fourth week of cross-country training, his running performance had notably deteriorated and he had lost eight pounds. He was 6'2" tall, weighed 147 pounds, and his estimated body fat composition was 6 per cent of his total body weight (a very low level).

Since a medical examination revealed no evidence of disease, the clue to his problems was sought through a review of his irregular eating habits. The patterns were clear. John would start the day with an hour's running before school, leaving him with no time for breakfast. His brown bag lunch consisted of a sandwich, an apple, and occasionally some cookies, all or part of which frequently did not get eaten because of his busy schedule. Returning home to dinner after a strenuous afternoon workout, he had little appetite, and what he did have was further dulled by parental urging to "eat a good dinner." His most significant and regular food intake came at night while doing his homework: typically, a peanut butter sandwich and milk.

His weight loss problem was easily explained. A growing 16-year-old boy cannot run ten miles every day and participate as a highly effective student on the energy and nutrient intake provided by such an unpredictable and casual diet. He like many athletes needed to know what constituted an adequate diet, and he needed to know the priority a good diet deserved in relation to his athletic, academic, and social responsibilities.

Specific recommendations for John were relatively simple. He was told the importance of "walking himself down" at the end of each run, providing continuing muscle movement after intense exercise. This would enhance his recovery from fatigue and help restore his appetite. And he would be expected to have more interest in his evening meal, if dinner were delayed for thirty or forty minutes after his arrival home.

The advantages of eating breakfast were discussed, but it was apparent that a sit-down breakfast at home was not in the realm of reality. Instead, a small can of fruit juice or a piece of fruit was added to his lunch bag, along with a breakfast roll or additional sandwich to be eaten between classes during the morning. His lunch was expanded to increase its caloric contribution, and an extra dessert was provided for consumption before the mid-afternoon workout. The evening meal consisted of generous servings of whatever the family was having for dinner; this, together with his earlier eating, provided all the essential nutrients. The balance of his energy needs were satisfied by late-evening snacks.

Two weeks after the original conference, John returned to the Clinic with a detailed ten-day record of his caloric consumption. During the early weeks of school it had been erratic, as low as 1500 Calories per day. With the prescribed diet it had increased, to as much as 4500 Calories per day. He felt energetic, was running better, and had gained four pounds. (Later in the season he was instructed on how to modify his normal diet in preparation for performing in district and state cross-country meets.)

John's experience is all too common. There are few teams without at least one or two members with such problems—deteriorating performance and accompanying weight loss. The solution must begin with the personal schedule of the athlete. Daily activities should be rearranged to provide pleasant associations and surroundings for eating. On this foundation sound dietary habits can be built.

The balance of this chapter will define a Basic Diet, one that provides the essentials for any athlete, and forms the basis upon which specific modifications for particular sports can be planned.

NUTRITIONAL REQUIREMENTS
FOR HEALTHY INDIVIDUALS

Fifty of the country's leading nutritional experts were called together in the early 1940's, concerned about the large number of young men being found unfit for military service (in World War II) because of nutrition-related health problems. Aware that a low level of nutritional health could threaten the war effort, the nation's leaders had asked the assembled group to define nutrient requirements for the American people. This group (known as the Food and Nutrition Board of the National Research Council of the National Academy of Sciences, a non-governmental, scientific body) published at the end of their deliberations a report known as the "Recommended Dietary Allowances," or RDA. The recommended allowances were listed for both males and females, who were categorized by age groups, with special considerations given for pregnancy and lactation.

The word "allowance" was chosen advisedly. The recommended allowances, the RDA, are not to be interpreted as definitive nutrient requirements, nor are they even recommended intakes for any particular person. They provide an informed guideline for planning and evaluating food intake, outlining the nutrient levels that will provide for the nutritional needs of essentially all normal, healthy people in the United States. It was implicit from the first that the RDA would be periodically reviewed and revised to keep up with advances in nutrition knowledge and changing American lifestyles. The allowances have been revised seven times, most recently in 1974. (A summary table of the current RDA is provided in Appendix A.)

The tables do not directly answer the questions of athletes (or their parents or coaches) as to what constitutes an appropriate basic daily diet. These allowances for nutrient intake must be converted into meaningful food recommendations. This problem concerned home economists and nutritionists when the RDA were first defined. As a result, nutritionists set about translating the RDA into terms that would be useful to most Americans in making their food choices.

In order to do this they identified certain groups of foods, each of which, if represented in the daily diet, would make a major and predictable contribution toward satisfying the need for a given nutrient, or group of related nutrients. These food groups were codified in a plan for daily intake and meal planning. This original plan was developed by the National Wartime Nutrition Program of the Department of Agriculture; it was widely disseminated as part of the war effort, and became known as the "Basic Seven Food Plan."[1]

In subsequent years, with advancing nutrition knowledge and a more uniform food supply throughout the country, it became evident that the Basic Seven Food Plan was unnecessarily complex, and in 1956 the Department of Agriculture's publication, "The Essentials of an Adequate Diet," described a more simplified diet guide based on a Four Food Group Plan.

THE FOUR FOOD GROUP PLAN

The Four Food Group Plan can readily be used to advantage by athletes, and by their parents, coaches and trainers. It has almost limitless flexibility, is particularly well suited to the American food supply, and is easy to communicate to athletic team members. It is the basis of nutrition education in essentially all primary and secondary schools, as well as in most public programs of nutrition education. The majority of Americans involved in athletics have probably had some exposure to the Four Food Group concept, but are seldom motivated to use it.

Each of the four food groups is composed of common food items that have been grouped together because of the common nutrient contributions they make to the diet. The four food groups are:

1. Milk and Milk Products

2. Meat and High-Protein Foods

3. Fruits and Vegetables

4. Cereal and Grain Foods

[1] A quick examination of the RDA table shows that the allowances are greatest for adolescent boys and girls. Growth requires both energy and building materials; and the extraordinarily large nutrient needs of the adolescent should heighten the concern for their nutritional health. During this period the growth of lean body tissues (blood, muscles, bones, organ tissues, etc.) is almost twice as large for boys as for girls, and the RDA tables reflect this difference.

The Milk and Milk Products Group

Each adult should receive the equivalent of two servings from the milk group each day—either drunk directly as a beverage, included in the preparation of other foods, or as alternate milk products (such as cheeses and ice cream). It may be desirable for some adolescents to have as many as three servings, depending on their age, growth rate, and the food choices that make up the remainder of their diet.

Milk products provide a particularly rich source of protein, calcium, and riboflavin (vitamin B_2). Yet with all its virtues, milk can be drunk to excess. Young American men and women are particularly prone to excessive milk-drinking habits. This drinking of large quantities of milk often tends to displace other important foods; and may add an excess of animal fat, protein, salt, and electrolytes to the diet. Young athletes drinking more than two glasses of milk each day would be well advised to drink skimmed, fortified milk. Unmodified milk products, particularly cheeses made with whole milk, are high in animal fat, salt, and calories.

In addition to contributing other nutrients, milk, particularly fortified powdered milk, can be an economical source of high-quality protein.

The Meat and High-Protein Food Group

This group includes meat, fish, poultry, eggs, and such alternate vegetable items as dried beans, peas, and nuts. In addition to their protein contribution, these foods are a major source of the B-group vitamins and iron. They are rich in readily absorbed iron themselves, and they increase the availability of the iron in any vegetable foods eaten with them.

Two or more servings from this group should be eaten each day. (A basic serving of meat is 3.5 ounces of the edible portion of the meat, a delicate serving for many hungry athletes.)

Because of concern over the saturated fat content of many meats and meat products, a "prudent" diet for Americans would limit intake of red meats to three or four servings per week, and eggs to three or four per week.[2] The remainder of the week's servings from this group should come from fish, chicken, and high-protein vegetable alternates such as beans, peas, and nuts.

Fruit and Vegetable Group

As the name indicates, this group consists of fruits and vegetables, including the potato; they are generally highly nutritious. Vegetables are particularly important sources of minerals and vitamins. Such leafy vegetables as spinach, lettuce, and cabbage also provide desired bulk in the form of undigestible cellulose. The citrus fruits, cantaloupe, strawberries, tomatoes, dark green leafy vegetables, and vegetables that are commonly eaten raw (such as cabbage and cauliflower) are significant sources of vitamin C and folic acid.

Four or more servings of fruit and vegetables should be included in the daily diet. When not served with butter or high-calorie salad dressings, their caloric density is relatively low, so they can be eaten in large amounts by people watching their weight.

If either fruit or a raw vegetable is not included in the diet, the daily allowances for vitamin C and folic acid (one of the B vitamins) will probably not be satisfied.

The Cereal and Grain Group

Bread, cereals, flour and baked goods are relatively inexpensive carbohydrate sources of energy. They also contribute protein, minerals, and a number of vitamins. (Whole grain cereal and cereal products, if prepared with enriched flours, provide significantly larger amounts of vitamins and minerals.)

Most people have little difficulty getting the recommended four daily servings from this group. The large active athlete, with high energy needs, will find here his most economical sources of energy.

[2]As noted in the last chapter, these are derived from the recommendations of the American Heart Association, and are offered as guidelines for the *general* population.

THE BASIC DIET PLAN

The recommended daily servings from the Four Food Groups are then: two servings each from the milk group and from the meat and protein-rich foods group, and four servings each from the cereal group and the fruit-and-vegetable group. These servings will of themselves supply essentially all necessary nutrients, no matter how large the athlete or how rigorous the training program.[3] But such a Basic Diet will *not* meet the energy (caloric) needs of a moderately active athlete, even a small one.

The energy contribution of the Basic Diet will vary, depending upon the selection of foods within the groups and the size of the servings, but it need not exceed 1200–1500 Calories per day. As a result, it can be used as an effective reducing diet, limiting caloric intake while supplying all essential nutrients.

What foods should be added to satisfy the needs for additional energy? Once the needs for essential nutrients have been satisfied, there's ample room for individual choice. An old axiom holds true: "First eat what you need and then eat what you want."

Most athletes respond by making their servings from the Four Food Groups much larger than the so-called "normal" servings. They also eat second and third helpings. Again, the word of caution is to limit the intake of animal fat. When high-calorie density foods (such as desserts) are used, the athlete should turn to items made with vegetable shortenings, to sherbets, and to milk drinks such as shakes and malts (which are usually made with fat-free dairy solids).

Lastly, the importance of water must be emphasized again. Available in abundance in this country, water is often overlooked as a most essential part of a daily diet. Yet few

---

[3]An important qualification must be noted with respect to iron. As will be discussed in Chapter 7, the iron requirement of girls and young women, after the onset of menstruation, may not be met by the Basic Diet. This can be a major health problem for girls involved in sports programs, and it demands special consideration.

The following are examples of Basic Diets:

5 MEALS

Breakfast

½ grapefruit
⅔ cup bran flakes
1 cup skim or low-fat milk
   or other beverage

Snack

1 small package raisins
½ bologna sandwich

Lunch

1 slice pizza
   carrot sticks
1 apple
1 cup skim or low-fat milk

Snack

2 oatmeal cookies

Dinner

   baked fish with
      mushrooms (3 oz.)
   baked potato
2 teasp. margarine
½ cup broccoli
1 cup tomato juice or skim
   or low-fat milk

Total calories: about 1400

3 MEALS

Breakfast

½ cup orange juice
1 soft-boiled or poached
   egg
1 slice whole wheat toast
1½ teasp. margarine
1 cup skim or low-fat milk
   or other beverage

Lunch

1½ cup Manhattan clam
   chowder
2 rye wafers
½ cup cottage cheese
   (uncreamed)
1 medium bunch grapes *or*
1 medium apple
1 granola cookie

Dinner

   oven barbecued chicken
      (3 oz., no bone)
½ cup green beans
½ cup cabbage and carrot
   salad
⅔ cup mashed potato
½ cup applesauce
1 cup skim or low-fat milk
   or other beverage

Total calories: about 1200

Alternate examples of Basic Diets can be found in Appendix B.

things can compromise athletic performance as effectively as an inadequate intake of water. Participation in even moderate exercise demands a minimum of a quart of fluid for every 1000 Calories of food. For a moderately active young person expending 3000 Calories per day, approximately three quarts of water are required. A large, very active athlete may need two to three times as much. The problem can become critical in warm and humid weather. It is therefore essential that the athlete develop water-drinking habits; soft drinks and milk are inadequate substitutes.

SUMMARY

In the past fifty years, nutrition science has provided numerical definition of the amounts of nutrients needed for the health maintenance of the "average" American. These so-called Recommended Dietary Allowances serve as guidelines for general day-to-day food planning and diet evaluation. While recognizing the wide variety of individual needs, they can be used as a realistic definition of a Basic Diet, the starting point for planning individual diets.

Translating these recommendations into menu items and food uses is done through the Four Food Group Plan. The Four Food Groups are: Milk and Milk Products, Meat and High-Protein Foods, Fruits and Vegetables, and Cereal and Grain Foods. By selecting specified numbers of servings from the various groups, one can obtain a diet with the requisite nutrients.

The Basic Diet, however, will not meet individual energy needs, particularly the needs of a high energy expending athlete. These needs must be met through additional food intake of larger servings and foods of individual preference. For certain very large and active individuals these additional food needs may be enormous.

The added calories should be provided by larger and more frequent servings of the food in the Basic Diet, as well as by high-calorie density foods, such as margarine, salad oils, and desserts. Individual likes and dislikes can be indulged, as long as intake is limited to a "prudent" amount of animal fat.

Preparation for many athletic activities will require special modification of this Basic Diet, particularly during periods preceding important competition.

But it must be remembered that the first essential in implementing any diet is to assure that food is made available with associations conducive to eating. The first real essential of a good diet is pleasant surroundings in which food will be eaten and enjoyed.

SUGGESTED READINGS AND REFERENCE WORKS

1. Recommended Dietary Allowances, 8th Ed. National Academy of Sciences, Wash. D.C., 1974.

2. Church, C.F. and Church, H.N.: *Food Values of Portions Commonly Used.* J.B. Lippincott Co., Phila., Pa., 1970.

3. Page, L. and Phippard, E.F.: *Essentials of an Adequate Diet.* Home Economics Research Report no. 3., Washington, D.C., U.S.D.A. Government Printing Office, 1957.

three

NONTRADITIONAL DIETS AND DIETARY SUPPLEMENTS

We live in an age of exploration. And as many, particularly the young, experiment with lifestyles, they inevitably are led to explore new ways of eating. Some of these are clearly healthy; others are not.

Most are some variation on the meatless diet. And it is often necessary to ask whether they are compatible with good health. Particularly, can an athlete perform well on a meatless diet?

We know, from the experiences of many cultures over the centuries, that meat is not a dietary essential. Vegetarian diets can and do support good health and active exercise, if selected with proper care. But in recent years rigidly restricted diets have been advocated which are conspicuously deficient in many nutrients, and they have been the cause of real nutrition problems.

VEGETARIAN AND OTHER MEATLESS DIETS

A very small number of people in the world eat a true vegetarian diet, restricted completely to fruits and vegetables. More commonly milk and milk products are also eaten in a so-called "lacto-vegetarian" diet. If eggs are included (a "lacto-ovo-vegetarian" diet), there is an even wider choice of foods to meet nutritional needs. The addition of milk and eggs is a particular advantage when the total amount of food eaten is limited, as in the diets of inactive young women. The milk and eggs provide relatively small quantities of certain essential amino acids, but these can be very important in complementing the amino acids of vegetable protein, and increasing their efficient utilization.

Anyone living on a meatless diet should follow a variant of the basic food selection principles described earlier with respect to the Basic Diet, i.e., the daily selection of food from designated food groups. The following shows a food group plan for the lacto-vegetarian diet, based on six food groups of vegetables, fruits, and milk and milk products. Eating one

---

ADDITIONAL SUGGESTIONS FOR NON-MEAT EATERS

Use a combination of beans; this will improve protein value. Add cooked beans to salads and soups; mash and combine with cheese for sandwich or taco filling.

Also eat a variety of cereal grains, for one protein complements another, increasing the value of both.

Four large mushrooms give ¼ of a day's allowance for niacin; slice them raw in salads.

One cup of prune juice supplies 55% of an adult woman's RDA for iron.

Sesame seeds can be made into candy squares. Prepare a thick syrup of brown sugar, margarine and water, add seeds, let cool and cut.

Eat sunflower seeds as a snack. They are a good source of protein and vitamins.

Brown sugar, honey, and syrup add calories and small amounts of minerals.

Sprinkle brewer's yeast, a vitamin B-complex source, in soups and cereals.

Add wheat germ to cooked cereal or sprinkle it over other foods. One-half ounce (2½ tablespoons) contains approximately three grams protein, plus iron and niacin.

to three daily servings from each of these food groups will satisfy essentially all nutritional requirements.

As indicated in relation to the Four Food Group Plan, some young women may not satisfy their needs for iron, unless their energy demands are unusually large and they take several servings of selected vegetables and fruits rich in iron. Young women with greater than normal iron demands, because of menstrual iron losses, often will require a medicinal iron supplement.

As with the Basic Diet, the meatless Six Food Group diet is designed to provide essential nutrients, but it does not necessarily satisfy the energy needs of an active individual. These needs can be more easily met with the use of certain meatless supplements—such as salad oils, nuts, and nut spreads—that have high caloric density.

There is one essential nutrient which is available only in food of animal origin. Unless milk, milk products, or eggs are included in the meatless diet, there will be no source of vitamin B_{12}. When this vitamin is lacking for a period of many months, anemia and muscle weakness may develop. A relatively small amount of milk, cheese, or eggs will satisfy the normal need for vitamin B_{12}.

DAILY FOOD GROUPS FOR LACTO-VEGETARIAN DIET*

I. FRUIT GROUP   Include daily three servings:

At least one serving of citrus or other fruit rich in Vitamin C. (Average value per serving = 50 mg.)

¼	cantaloupe	½	cup orange juice
½	grapefruit	1	cup red raspberries
½	cup grapefruit juice	1	cup strawberries
1	orange	1	cup tomato juice

At least one serving of fruit rich in iron. (Average value per serving = 4 mg.)

½	cup dried uncooked apricots	¾	cup cooked prunes
		½	cup prune juice

¾ cup dates	¾ cup raisins
7 large dried figs	¾ cup dried cooked peaches
½ cup dried uncooked peaches	

II. VEGETABLE GROUP   Include daily three servings:

At least one serving (½ cup) green or yellow vegetable (average value per serving = 5000 IU Vitamin A. Starred items contain average of 1.5 mg. iron per serving.

*Beet greens, cooked	Pumpkin, canned, cooked
Carrots, raw	*Mustard greens, cooked
Collards, cooked	*Spinach, cooked
*Kale, cooked	Squash, winter, baked

At least two ½ cup servings of other vegetables. Some suggestions:

Bean sprouts	Macaroni
Beets	Mushrooms
Broccoli	Noodles
Brussel sprouts	Onions
Cabbage	Potato
Cauliflower	Rice
Celery	Spaghetti
Cucumber	Tomatoes
Eggplant	Turnips
Green beans	
Lettuce	

III. MILK GROUP   Include daily three servings of milk and milk products. (Three servings supply an average of 0.8 gms. calcium, 1.2 mg. riboflavin, and 30 grams of protein.)

1½ oz. American cheese
1 cup buttermilk

*Modified from plan originally developed at Stanford University.

½ cup cottage cheese, creamed
2 cups ice cream
1 cup milk (skim, low fat, or whole)
1 cup plain yogurt made with low-fat milk

IV. PEAS AND BEANS　Include daily at least one serving:

Fresh　(¾ cup cooked provides an average value of 8 gms. protein, 2.5 mg. iron, 1.5 mg. niacin.)

Black-eyed peas	Lima beans
Green peas	Sprouted mung beans

Dried beans　(½ cup cooked provides an average value of 8 gms. protein, 2.2 mg. iron, .7 mg. niacin.)

Black-eyed peas	Soy beans
Great Northern beans	Split peas
Lima beans	Red kidney beans, canned
Navy beans	

V. NUTS　Include daily at least one serving (½ cup) of nuts or peanut butter. (¼ cup supplies average of 6 gms. protein, 1.7 mg. niacin, and 1.3 mg. iron.)

Almonds, shelled whole	Pecans, shelled halves
Cashew nuts, roasted	Walnuts, black
Peanuts, roasted	

Peanut butter (2 tablespoons supplies 8 gms. protein, 4.8 mg. niacin, and .6 mg. iron.

VI. BREADS AND CEREALS　Include daily at least three servings of bread (1 slice/serving) and cereals (¾ cup/serving). Whole wheat, other whole grains, or products made from enriched flours are good sources of B vitamins and iron, and provide two-to-three gms./protein in each serving.

A sample menu for the Lacto-Vegetarian Diet described above would be:

Morning		**SAMPLE**	
1	serving citrus fruit	½	grapefruit
1	serving bread	1	slice bread with margarine
1	serving cereal	1½	cups oatmeal with honey
1	serving milk	1	cup low-fat milk

Noon

½ cup cottage cheese
spinach salad with 2 T.
salad oil

½	serving milk
1	serving vegetable
1	serving bread	1 slice bread with margarine
1	serving fruit	1 banana

Snack

| 1 | serving milk | 1 cup low-fat milk |
| 1 | serving nuts | ½ cup peanuts |

Evening

1 cup cream of tomato soup

1	serving green or yellow vegetable	2 cups spaghetti with tomato sauce and cheese
1	serving potato or substitute	1 apple
½	serving milk	1 slice bread with margarine
1	serving fruit
1	serving bread

Snack

½ cup prune juice

1 serving fruit (rich in iron)

This diet provides approximately:

Calories	2550		Thiamine	1.6	mg
Protein	144	g	Riboflavin	2.6	mg
Fat	106	g	Niacin	20.3	mg
Carbohydrate	310	g	Vitamin C	115	mg
Calcium	1593	mg	Vitamin A	5335	IU
Iron	22	mg			

This menu will meet the nutrient needs of an active 160-to-170 pound athlete, except his needs for energy. No supplements are needed. Meeting energy needs can be accomplished by enlarging servings and adding (not substituting) preferred foods.

"First eat what you need (the menu)—then eat what you want."

A concerned coach, trainer, or parent may occasionally have doubts as to whether or not an athlete can compete optimally on a meatless diet. He can, as long as he follows the rules laid down above, choosing from a wide selection of foods each day, and, if the diet includes no foods of animal origin, adding a periodic supplement of vitamin B_{12}. Several world-class athletes have competed very successfully on such meatless diets.

NONCONVENTIONAL DIETS INCOMPATIBLE WITH HEALTH AND GOOD ATHLETIC PERFORMANCE

Several recently popular diets limit food choice to one or two food groups, and therefore exclude many essential nutrients. Perhaps the best known is the Zen Macrobiotic Diet. It involves a series of ten diets, progressing from the lowest level, minus 3, which allows 30 per cent animal products, to the highest level, 7, which consists entirely of cereal and restricted amounts of fluids. Not surprisingly, disciples of this diet have developed a whole spectrum of nutritional problems, from mild starvation to death. Such extreme dietary practices among young athletes usually call for medical (and perhaps psychiatric) consultation.

Less immediately threatening is a Fruitarian Diet, which is limited to raw and dried fruits, nuts, honey, and olive oil. These foods are highly nutritious, but they do not contain all essential nutrients. And athletic performance (as well as general health) will suffer, if specific provision is not made to supply missing nutrients through a broader selection of vegetables and grains.

Now and then a question arises regarding the advantages of periodic fasting. Fasting limited to 24 or 48 hours need not be damaging to a healthy individual, but an athlete cannot expect to compete effectively if he is deprived of energy sources for such periods during his training. There is no evidence to suggest that periodic fasting provides any competitive advantage.

It is obvious from what has been said that good health and optimal athletic performance do not require a "traditional" diet. There are many opportunities for exploring various dietary experiences in connection with new lifestyles. But basic needs must be met. And this is best accomplished by following a food group guideline, and thereby eating foods which supply essential nutrients and sufficient energy.

Organic Foods

Growing interest in nutrition, new diets, and food safety has prompted a widespread use of so-called "organic" and related "health" foods. Of course all foods are organic in a chemical sense, but the term "organic food" is now commonly used to mean foods grown and processed without the use of "chemicals." Proponents claim health, flavor, and ecological advantages.

There is no sound scientific evidence that either taste or nutrient quality of food is affected by the nature of the fertilizer used in its production. On the other hand, safety may be adversely affected. Since organic foods are often grown and marketed locally, often they may not be subjected to many of the safety regulations that are applied to the conventional food supply involved in interstate commerce. The safety of the conventional food supply in the United States is more effectively regulated today than ever before in history.

Modern agricultural technology, including the use of agricultural chemicals in food production and preservation, plays an essential role in efforts to provide for the world's food needs. It can help young athletes meet their large food demands safely and economically. And although eating adventures with so-called "health" or "natural" foods may add interest to the diet, there is no justification in terms of nutrition or safety; there is no need to part from conventional food sources.

Weight Control Diets

Millions of dollars are spent in the United States each year on schemes alleged to insure quick and effortless loss of weight. Most of them say nothing about increasing exercise. They simply recommend bizarre and severely restricted diets. Classic examples are the "grapefruit diet," the "fried chicken diet," and the "drinking man's diet." Nutritionally, they are grossly inadequate. The only saving grace is that their potential harm is limited by their unattractiveness; most often people can't stay on them long enough to develop serious nutritional deficiencies.

A book published in 1972, *Dr. Atkins' Diet Revolution*, has been used by some athletes in attempts to lose weight. Dr. Atkins' diet allows an unrestricted intake of calories from protein and fat, and in fact encourages a high intake of saturated fats and cholesterol-rich foods. Carbohydrates are rigidly restricted. This very unusual diet is particularly hazardous for the athlete and warrants particular mention.

Metabolizing a large amount of fatty acids will produce ketosis, which in turn can produce fatigue, dehydration, nausea, and alterations in heart rate, and can contribute to dehydration. Physically active people are most susceptible. Several groups of high school wrestlers have tried to control their weight with Dr. Atkins' diet, at marked jeopardy to their health and athletic performance.

VITAMIN SUPPLEMENTS

It has been said that American athletes have the most expensive urine in the world. The reason is their tendency to use massive doses of vitamin supplements which far exceed their needs. The water-soluble vitamins that the body cannot use are rapidly excreted in the urine. (As pointed out below, fat-soluble vitamins taken in mass are retained in the body.)

Is there a need for vitamin supplements in the diet of the competitive athlete? The answer is no, not if his diet includes a proper variety of foods. Nevertheless, the widespread use of such supplements by well-nourished American athletes has reached ridiculous proportions.

Take the recent example of a varsity crew in intense training for the rowing season. All the oarsmen weighed over 200 pounds, all were over six feet tall, and all were eating at a training table. During the training period, they each consumed between 5000 and 6000 Calories per day. Their diet was ample, professionally supervised, and actually contained several times the amount of vitamins and protein they needed for optimal health and performance. Yet each of the oarsmen was taking five different nutritional supplements each day. More than once a day each took a high-potency multi-vitamin capsule, a rose hips vitamin C capsule, a "High Energol" capsule, a vitamin E capsule and a vitamin B-complex capsule. The supplements were completely worthless and represented (over the season) several hundred dollars of needless expense.

A disturbing level of nutritional ignorance supports the market for such things as the "High Energol" capsules, taken, as the name implies, for energy. According to the label, the recommended dose of six capsules each day provides a total of 84 kilo-calories. This is equal to the energy contribution of a small glass of Coca-Cola and less than that of a piece of buttered toast.

Not only are the supplements worthless, they can conceivably prove harmful. The fat-soluble vitamins (A, D, E, and K) provided by the multi-vitamin capsule cannot be excreted in the urine and are instead stored in body fat, principally in the liver. Over a significant period of time, this build-up of excess vitamins can produce serious toxic effects, particularly through an accumulation of vitamins A and D.

Vitamin supplementation is often abused by athletes under the misconception that if a little is good, more will be better. As mentioned earlier vitamins function in regulating metabolic body processes; they do not contribute energy. Increasing energy demands and energy expenditure does *not* increase the demand for vitamins (with the exception of thiamine, which is adequately supplied in the normal diet).

It is relevant to consider the Recommended Dietary Allowance for vitamins in the Appendix. It shows that the allowance for vitamins varies only slightly among different ages, sizes, and sexes. To put it simply, a large, active man does not require significantly more vitamins than a small, sedentary woman. Even in pregnancy and lactation, the most demanding nutritional experiences, the increased need for vitamins is minimal.

As stated earlier, a diet providing no more than 1200 to 1500 Calories, if properly selected from traditional American foods, will provide all the vitamins and protein anybody needs.

Vitamins E and C

Two vitamins deserve special consideration, since they are commonly taken as supplements in very large amounts. The first of these is vitamin E. In an earlier chapter it was pointed out that certain of the vitamins, such as biotin, pantothenic acid of the B group, and vitamin E, are required in such minute amounts that even the worst of diets ordinarily supplies all the body can use. In other words, medical science has not found significant evidence that deficiencies of these nutrients exist. Yet millions of people, and especially athletes, spend enormous amounts of money on vitamin E capsules, solutions, fortifiers, skin lotions, etc.—all unnecessary and useless. Supplements of vitamin E do *not* increase stamina, do *not* improve circulation or delivery of oxygen to muscles, do *not* lower blood cholesterol, do *not* prevent graying of hair, and, perhaps of most interest, do *not* enhance sexual potency or cure infertility.

Some years ago, after considerable effort in elaborate nutrition experiments, a group of researchers succeeded in devising a vitamin E-deficient diet, which was fed to rats. Among other symptoms, the rats exhibited evidence of sterility. When vitamin E was returned to their diet, they became potent again. It was indeed tempting to postulate that the experiment had revealed the answer to one of man's eternal goals: increased sexual potency. Unfortunately, this did not prove to be the case. Modern man does not develop vitamin E deficiency, and taking supplemental doses has no effect on his sexual potency or performance. (This is but one of many examples where laboratory findings with rats cannot be usefully extrapolated to humans.)

Vitamin C is also commonly taken in large amounts. The Basic Diet supplies the very generous RDA of this vitamin, and accordingly, supplementation is not needed by anyone on a well-selected diet. But controversy has recently arisen over the efficacy of vitamin C in preventing and alleviating the symptoms of the common cold. It has been suggested by some that vitamin C is effective in preventing or shortening the duration of cold symptoms, if taken in doses of 10 to 100 times the amounts available in the most nutritious diet. (When taken in such quantities, one is really not considering a dietary supplement but the use of a nutrient as a drug or medication.)

Several well-designed clinical experiments have been conducted to evaluate the effectiveness of this claim. At present the available evidence indicates that in doses that might be considered safe for use, vitamin C reduces neither the frequency nor the duration of the common cold sufficiently to justify its use by healthy individuals. In any event, dosage should be restricted to well below the levels suggested by the vitamin's most fervent advocates.

Although long-term studies have not been completed to show whether there are any adverse reactions to doses of 1000 to 1500 mgs. per day, these levels are generally regarded as safe. There is no verification that an increase beyond these levels serves any useful purpose. And, since any harmful effect could be expected to increase proportionately with the dosage, 1500 mgs. per day should probably be considered the upper limit.

In fact, there is really no substantial evidence justifying dosage at those levels, or even beyond the recommended dietary allowance of 45 mgs. per day. Traditional hygienic practices, such as hand-washing, getting sufficient sleep, and maintaining good fluid intake will probably accomplish much more in minimizing the risk of colds.

PROTEIN SUPPLEMENTS

Hoping to increase body size and strength, many athletes have been attracted to high-protein diets and concentrated protein supplements. This blind belief in protein (usually under-cooked animal protein) goes back well before the advent of modern nutritional science. The theory persists today. The use of high-protein diets, supplemented by high-protein drinks and powders, is widespread among certain groups of athletes, even though their diets ordinarily contain three or four times what the body needs for optimal performance.

It is worth repeating that the Basic Diet provides abundant protein. In addition, many foods preferred by athletes as energy supplements to the Basic Diet, particularly dairy products, soy products, and nuts, contain large amounts of high-quality protein. There are drawbacks to uncontrolled protein intakes in the diet, in addition to the needless expense. It is the least efficient source of energy; and, as mentioned earlier, high-protein diets are dehydrating, because they demand large amounts of water for urinary excretion of the metabolic by-products. When taken in excessive amounts, protein supplements may also cause loss of appetite and diarrhea.

Typical of many of the popular protein supplements is a product called "Super 96 Protein," which one conscientious football player took while attempting to gain weight. Instead it ruined his appetite and produced severe diarrhea, resulting in actual weight loss. The label of Super 96 Protein indicates that it contains animal protein from, among other sources, "undenatured liver, pancreas, heart, spleen, mammary, ovarian and testicular substance." This long list of slaughterhouse refuse certainly has no place in the diet of any individual, especially a healthy athlete trying to maintain a good appetite and a sound level of hydration.

SUMMARY

Meatless diets can meet the needs of the largest and most vigorous athletes (except energy), if the diet is properly selected from the six groups of fruits and vegetables. Adding milk, milk products, and eggs will increase the efficiency of protein use, and add variety and caloric density.

Severely restricted diets are most apt to be nutritionally inadequate. Some, such as the Zen Macrobiotic Diet, represent new adventures in lifestyles. Others, like Dr. Atkins' ketogenic diet, promise an easy route to weight loss through bizarre eating restrictions. These diets, over long periods of time, will lead to severe undernutrition. They are hazardous in any athletic training program.

The use of so-called "organic" foods ordinarily causes no harm. But they provide no nutritional, taste, or safety advantages and are often unduly expensive.

Among American athletes' least desirable dietary practices is the use of expensive, useless, and potentially dangerous vitamin and protein supplements. The athlete's need for essential nutrients is adequately met by the Basic Diet, supplemented for needed energy by conventional foods of his personal preference.

SUGGESTED READINGS AND REFERENCE WORKS

1. Wolff, R.J.: "Who Eats for Health?"*Am. J. Clin. Nutrit.*, 26:438, 1973.

2. Erhard, D.: "Nutrition Education for the New Generation." *J. of Nutrit. Ed.,* p. 135, Spring, 1971.

3. Ellis, F.R. and Montignffo, V.M.E.:" Veganism, Clinical findings and investigations." *Am. J. Clin. Nutr.,* 23:249, 1970.

4. Darden, E.: "Questions and Answers on Health Foods for Athletes." *Coach* 44:68, 1975.

5. Report of the Council on Food and Nutrition of the American Medical Association: A critique of Low Carbohydrate Ketogenic Weight Reduction Regimens. A Review of Dr. Atkins' Diet Revolution.

four

GAINING
OR LOSING
WEIGHT

Conceptually nothing could be more simple than gaining or losing weight. To lose weight, you have to expend more energy (calories) than you ingest. Gaining weight requires just the opposite. It all seems an easy matter of energy balance. But if that's true, why the difficulty?

Weight problems among athletes are common, and with a better understanding of the principles involved, they can be solved. This can't be done with the sudden starvation or glutting that so often precedes the ceremonial march to the scales. Weight-change programs must be carefully planned and developed from a clear recognition of how and why the body loses or gains weight. A basic understanding of energy, and its relationship to body input (food) and output (energy expenditure), provides an excellent starting point.

HOW ENERGY IS MEASURED

The energy sources in food, as well as the body's energy expenditure, are conventionally measured in units of heat expressed as "calories." The calorie is the amount of heat required to raise the temperature of one gram of water one degree centigrade. This is a very small unit of heat and is convenient for use in the laboratory. When dealing with energy in food and in human energy expenditure, a more suitable unit is the kilo-calorie. One kilo-calorie is equivalent to 1000 calories; and common usage has been adopted in this book, with "Calorie" (with a capital "C") referring to the kilo-calorie.

THE BODY'S USE OF ENERGY

Man gets his energy in chemical form, through the food he eats. It is utilized to meet a variety of body needs, including physical work and the physical activity associated with athletic performance. Energy is used to maintain body temperature; it is required for the growth of new tissues, which is greatest during the growing years of adolescence; and it is needed for a variety of organ functions: the work of the heart in pumping blood, the work of muscles in breathing and during digestion, and the maintenance of the proper chemical balance within the body cells.

MAN'S ENERGY EXPENDITURE

When we are completely at rest and have not eaten for at least 12 hours, we are using energy only to keep internal organs functioning and to maintain body temperature. This so-called "basal" energy expenditure, or "basal metabolism," goes on day in and day out, throughout the entire 24 hours of the day. And in order to maintain a given weight our energy intake (from food measured in calories) must equal our basal energy expenditure *plus* that expended through physical activity.

The basal energy needs of a man six feet tall and weighing 175 pounds are approximately 1800 Calories a day. His age, sex, size, and his degree of fatness, all influence his basal rate. Since fat tissue is metabolically much less active than muscle and organ tissue, a muscular person will expend more energy when at rest than a person of the same weight with a larger proportion of body fat. As a result, women (with a larger percentage of fat) generally have a lower rate of basal metabolism.

The effect of age on basal metabolism is also important. There is a significant decline in basal energy expenditure with increasing age. Consequently, a person with very large energy and food needs during adolescence may have rather modest needs when middle-aged. Between the ages of 25 and 35, daily basal needs will decrease an average of approximately 50 Calories; and they will fall a total of about 150 Calories between the ages of 35 and 55. Although this may not seem like a significant amount, if an appropriate reduction in food intake is not made, the cumulative result would be 15 pounds of body fat each year. The basal energy requirement goes down at the very time most people are becoming less physically active (and generally more affluent). Since they often do not compensate by reducing their caloric intake, the result can only be obesity—a very common problem in our adult population.

Basal energy expenditure is also affected by the amount and type of food that is eaten. When an individual eats a meal, there is an immediate expenditure of energy in the digestion and metabolism of the consumed food. This is known as "specific dynamic action," and the energy involved will vary with the type of food eaten. Metabolic activity is most active following ingestion and metabolism of protein foods. An individual eating a meal of pure protein may utilize in the metabolic process (through specific dynamic action) as much as 30 per cent of the calories in the eaten food. This phenomenon has given credence to a gross overstatement commonly made by advocates of high-protein reducing diets: that the dieter can eat as much protein as he wants, because the specific dynamic action will use up all the calories. Not only is the arithmetic bad, the theory also overlooks the fact that most so-called "high-protein" foods in the American diet are also very high in fat content.

ENERGY EXPENDITURE
IN VARIOUS SPORTS

In estimating total energy needs, we must add to the basal energy expenditure the calories that are used up in various forms of physical activity. The size of an individual and the speed and vigor with which the activity is pursued all affect the amount of energy expended. For example, a 187-pound man walking at two miles an hour may burn approximately 200 Calories in an hour's walk. If he walks a brisk four miles an hour, his caloric expenditure will double to nearly 400 Calories in the same period of time. A larger man walking at the same rate will expend more, a smaller man less.

The following table shows approximate energy expenditures for a variety of activities. Since two individuals may expend greatly differing amounts of energy while participating in the same game, this table can give only rough estimates.

There are more precise methods of determining caloric expenditure during athletic activity. One method is through

RECREATIONAL ENERGY EXPENDITURE
(in Calories per minute)

Sitting—bridge	1.5-2
Walking level	3-5 (3mph)
Canoeing (4mph)	3-7
Volleyball	3-10
Playing with children	3.5-10
Cycling (13mph)	4-11
Golf	5
Archery	5
Dancing	5-7
Swimming	5-10
Tennis	7-10
Touch football	7-10
Squash	10-12
Cross-country	10-15
Skiing	15
Climbing	11-12
Running (10mph)	18-20

(Astrand, P. O., and Roclabl, K. *Textbook of Work Physiology*. McGraw-Hill, New York, 1970. Chapter 13, p. 439.)

prescription of a specific diet of known caloric content. For example, one can weigh an individual for whom a 3000-Calorie diet is prescribed. After two to three weeks, he is again weighed and it can be readily determined whether the dieter has been expending more or less than the 3000 Calories contained in his diet.

Probably the simplest and most commonly used method to determine caloric expenditure is to ask an individual to follow his normal dietary pattern and to record all food that he eats. From these food records the caloric intake can be calculated. The subject should also be periodically weighed, but usually there is no significant weight change during the two to three weeks required to get a reliable documentation of his caloric intake.

Most people maintain a relatively constant body weight in adulthood, restricting caloric intake to amounts commensurate with their energy needs. The expenditure of energy normally prompts food intake, but seldom is the reverse true. Only in the case of real starvation, when energy from food is not available, does the body decrease its expenditure of energy and refuse to do muscular work. And tragic as it is in a society faced with widespread problems of obesity, high energy intake does not prompt high energy expenditure.

THE ENERGY CONTRIBUTION OF VARIOUS FOODS

The amount of calories in a given food can be determined by the amount of heat given off when that food is combusted. If one makes the appropriate allowance for how efficiently the food is digested and metabolized (its specific dynamic action), and whether or not there is significant loss of nutrient in the urine, it is possible to determine the effective energy contribution of foods or food mixtures. And using this information for food selection is essential in planning any weight-change diet.

In the early part of this century an apparatus was devised in which food could be completely combusted, and the released heat could be measured with great precision. This instrument was called the "calorimeter."

It was discovered that when a gram of fat was combusted, the amount of heat (energy) liberated was between 9.1 and 9.4 Calories. Since approximately 95 per cent of the fat we eat is absorbed during digestion, and none is excreted, each gram of fat contributes about 9 Calories of energy.

When carbohydrate was combusted, 4.1 Calories of heat energy were liberated. Since better than 99 per cent of food carbohydrate is absorbed and none is lost, each gram of carbohydrate contributes about 4 Calories of energy, less than half of that contributed by a gram of fat. When protein was combusted, 5.5 Calories were produced. However, only 92 per cent of protein is absorbed in the digestion process, and certain metabolic by-products (approximately 1.25 Calories per gram of protein) are excreted in the urine. Therefore, each gram of protein contributes only about 4 Calories of effective energy (the same as for carbohydrates). Alcohol, which has been studied in the same way, is absorbed completely, and each gram contributes 7 Calories of energy.

The 9 Calories per gram of fat represent the most concentrated form of food energy. In practical terms, 3500 Calories of energy, the amount that may be needed daily by an active young athlete, would be found in almost a full pound of pure fat. Recognizing this fact, the fraud of the high-energy capsules, often marketed specifically for athletes, becomes quite obvious. Capsules weighing at most a few grams cannot possibly make a significant energy contribution to the needs of the athlete. Even if these capsules represented the most concentrated form of energy usable by the body (that of pure oil or fat), their caloric contribution would be very limited. Their weight in grams, multiplied by nine (the number of Calories contributed by a gram of fat), gives their total caloric content. Since one teaspoon of fat weighs approximately 5 grams, it contributes no more than 45 Calories. Assuming

that a high-energy capsule weighed 5 grams (certainly gargan-
tuan for a capsule), its caloric contribution would also be
45 Calories. And that is the energy available from about half
of a typical cola drink.

The athlete with high energy demands may find it helpful to include in his diet generous amounts of fatty foods.
This is particularly true for the young competitor in energy-
demanding sports, like basketball, soccer, and distance running, who can reduce the total bulk of his diet by including
larger amounts of fat and still meet his energy needs. Margarine, nuts, and nutspreads such as peanut butter and vegetable oils all add concentrated calories without an unnecessary
addition of bulk or saturated animal fats. The high caloric
intakes necessary for weight gain by many athletes must
usually include the calories contained in fats. An example
of a very high-caloric diet, containing little animal fat,
comes later in this chapter, and there are alternates in the
Appendix.

As indicated, carbohydrates provide 4 Calories of energy
per gram, less than half that of fats. Nonetheless, starches
and sweets may contribute a lot of calories to the diet and
are often considered "fattening." They do provide a significant
amount of energy, because they are made from refined carbohydrate sources like table sugar and highly milled flour.
They also have minimal water and fiber content, and are,
therefore, relatively concentrated sources of calories. Popular
desserts like pies, cakes, and pastries, which are customarily
thought of as being carbohydrate foods, actually contain large
amounts of shortening, which is fat and accounts for much
of their caloric contribution. Other carbohydrate foods, like
spaghetti, noodles, potatoes, and rice, contribute fewer calories,
unless eaten in very large amounts or in combination with
fatty foods.

Certain vegetables, such as celery, lettuce, and cabbage,
contain large amounts of carbohydrate in the form of cellulose,
but provide very little energy. Humans cannot digest cellulose,
and it only adds bulk to the diet. In fact, foods high in cellulose
are excellent for people who must restrict their caloric intake.

But, because of their high bulk and low caloric content, they are inefficient for those who have high energy demands.

As mentioned in an earlier chapter, protein is the least efficient of the three energy sources in the diet. Although protein provides 4 Calories of energy per gram, the manner in which it is metabolized greatly reduces the availability of the energy it supplies. Before protein can be utilized for energy it must be converted to glucose, a metabolic process which in itself demands significant amounts of energy. Additional energy is dissipated in the urinary excretion of metabolic by-products. As a result, when athletes consume more protein than they actually need, the additional protein is an inefficient energy source.

Alcohol is a poor source of energy under any circumstance. It has a depressing effect on the central nervous system, has a dehydrating influence, and must be converted into glucose by the liver before its energy can be made available for muscle work. It's important to recognize that the conversion of alcohol to glucose takes place only in the liver and goes on very slowly. Muscles cannot use alcohol as a direct source of energy. And the practice of exercising to hasten the metabolism of alcohol ("walking off" an intoxicating dose) is of no help and may actually be dangerous.

ALTERING ENERGY BALANCE

In gaining or losing weight, man must obey the first law of thermodynamics: he can neither create nor destroy energy, but can only transform it from one form to another. Thus food energy taken in excess of that required for basal metabolism and physical activity must be stored, usually as fat. Once stored as excess body fat, energy can only be disposed of through conversion to some other energy form, specifically the work energy of physical activity.

Knowing the potential energy stored in one gram of fat (9 Calories), we can readily convert from grams to pounds and calculate that a pound of fat represents approximately 4000 Calories. When allowance is made for the other tissue elements in fat tissue, it can be estimated that one pound of fat represents a storage of about 3500 Calories of energy. Lean body tissue, such as muscle, contains less fat, more protein, and more water, and represents approximately 2500 Calories of potential energy.

These estimates are very approximate, but they can be useful in diet planning. For example, *to gain one pound in the form of muscle mass, an excess of approximately 2500 Calories will be needed. To lose one pound of fat, on the other hand, approximately 3500 Calories of energy must be expended in excess of that taken in in the diet.*

Gaining Weight

For many athletes gaining weight is a real and difficult problem. There are obvious contact sports, such as football and hockey, where added weight is often valued. But the problem of gaining or maintaining weight is rather widespread. In swimming and basketball, for instance, where training and competitive seasons are long and arduous, many athletes have difficulty reaching or maintaining their "ideal" weight, to the detriment of their performance.

The difficulty is often one of underestimating just how many calories are required by the active competitor, in terms of the kinds and quantities of food which must be eaten. When one thinks of "fattening" foods, something like beer or potatoes comes to mind. These foods provide considerable energy, but they will not help an athlete gain weight, because they are not high in caloric density—bulky in relation to the number of calories they represent.

Take the recent experience of a young man who decided to gain weight by drinking beer. Every evening he managed to get down about 14 bottles of beer. Yet in spite of the popular images of beer-bellied folks in Milwaukee, he was not gaining weight. As a matter of fact, it was an inefficient way to get his calories. He was burning up approximately 6000 Calories a day; and the 1700 Calories represented by the beer (which eliminated his appetite for the day) were clearly not enough.

The amount of energy expended by a typical young male athlete in training, up to as much as 5000 to 6000 Calories per day, represents the energy contribution of a large diet. If he is trying to gain weight, his caloric intake must become very significant indeed. At a rate of 2500 Calories per pound of muscle mass, an athlete must exceed his caloric expenditure by nearly 1000 Calories per day if he wishes to gain as much as two pounds per week (figuring 5 effective training days in a week). For a large active athlete, this could add up to a total requirement of 6500 to 7500 Calories per day. And that takes both knowledge of the principles involved and a well-devised diet program.[1]

The starting place is a careful record of all food eaten for one week. By analyzing the record, the athlete can determine his regular caloric intake, which usually will be the amount necessary to maintain his present weight. Often he will be amazed to discover how great a caloric requirement he has. The food record will also show individual likes and dislikes. And these are important. As is true with any diet program, but perhaps most critically true in setting up a high-calorie diet, desired foods must be emphasized or the diet can't be maintained.

The following 6000-Calorie diet was recently devised for a football player who hoped to gain weight during a summer period of training and conditioning. It clearly shows the large amount of food required to reach the caloric levels needed by large, active young people in order to gain weight. This diet requires six meals a day.

Note that large-bulk foods—cereals and grains, beverages, salads, and the like—are not emphasized. They can be very important sources of nutrients for people on low-calorie diets, but they are too filling relative to caloric contribution for this diet. In the main, fats, which have a high caloric density, are included in the form of vegetable oils. Again, it is essential

---

[1] No athlete should be encouraged to participate in a weight-gaining program if he has a family medical history of heart disease. In addition, a blood examination should always be given to determine whether or not there are abnormal levels of plasma lipids.

HIGH CALORIE DIET: 6,000 CALORIES (6 MEALS)

Breakfast

½ cup orange juice
1 cup oatmeal
1 cup low-fat milk
1 scrambled egg
1 slice whole wheat toast
1½ teasp. margarine
1 tablespoon jam

Total Calories: 665

Lunch

5 fish sticks
  tartar sauce
  large serving, French fries
  green salad with avocado
    and French dressing
1 cup lemon sherbet
2 granola cookies
1 cup low-fat milk

Total Calories: 1505

Dinner

1 cup cream of mushroom
    soup
2 pieces oven baked
    chicken
  candied sweet potato
1 dinner roll and
    margarine
1 cup carrots and peas
½ cup coleslaw
1 piece cherry pie
  beverage

Total Calories: 1615

Snack

1 peanut butter sandwich
1 banana
1 cup grape juice

Total Calories: 485

Snack

1 cup mixed dried fruit
1½ cup malted milk

Total Calories: 660

Snack

1 cup cashew nuts
1 cup cocoa

Total Calories: 1045

Daily Total Calories: 5975

that excessive amounts of animal fats be avoided; in addition to the health problems they pose, there is the feeling of satiety, of fullness, that they provide. There should be an abundance of low-bulk carbohydrates, rich in energy, economical, and usually enjoyable.

A realistic time schedule is important in any weight-gaining program. Since 2500 Calories in excess of needs are required to gain one pound of lean body weight, an active athlete, one for example who expends 4000 Calories a day, can gain approximately two to three pounds each week if he is able to ingest a 5000-Calorie diet. (*It is important that caloric intake not exceed expenditure by more than 1000 to 1500 Calories per day, if accumulation of excess fat is to be avoided.*)

The athlete usually wants to make sure that any added weight is primarily in lean body mass, not fat. The high-calorie diet must therefore be accompanied by a vigorous training program. Weight gain should be monitored by measuring skin folds at different body sites and at regular intervals. (More on this later in the chapter and in the Appendix.) This will insure that exercise is sufficient to build body muscle and that the increase in weight is not merely in the form of fat. In addition, when calorie intakes are at these high levels, abundant protein will be present to provide the amino acid building blocks for new lean body tissue.

As a general proposition carbohydrate foods are less expensive than those rich in animal protein. The sample diets furnished in this book provide economic alternatives for making the best use of the resources available. However, the costs of large weight-gaining diets can be great, and coaches and administrators should be sensitive to this factor. They may need to provide scholarship funds—or make training tables available to athletes who can't afford the cost.

Promoting Weight Gain With Androgen Hormones. It has been repeatedly demonstrated that the administration of male sex hormone, testosterone, and of synthetic anabolic agents such as Dianabol, will result in an increase in muscle tissue—if accompanied by a vigorous conditioning program and a high-calorie diet. There is no agreement as to whether strength, endurance, or athletic performance will be improved. (The increase in muscle mass has been real, but the effect on performance is difficult to document in many sports.) In any case, these hormone agents and their derivatives are frequently used by athletes, particularly those involved in such sports as weight-lifting, football, and wrestling. In the opinion of most, diet management and training, without the use of hormones, can produce essentially the same results.

But the question of whether or not these hormones have positive effects is academic, in the light of the ethical and nutritional considerations. Anyone who takes anabolic steroids before he or she stops growing will have growth stunted (through the premature arrest of the growth zones at the end of long bones). Many who take them for as long as a few weeks develop acne, deepening of the voice, excessive body hair, and enlargement of the breasts (because some of the hormones are converted to the female hormone, estrogen). And, in cases where anabolic agents are administered to males after growth has stopped, generally after the ages of 18 to 20, the most serious problems relate to testicular structure and function. In studies in which these agents were administered for periods of from 8 to 25 weeks, there was uniform evidence of diminished testicular size, loss of potency, and marked decrease in sperm production. Even after recovery from the other side effects, evidence of altered sperm production persisted.

It is obvious that the use of these hormones by healthy individuals is never justified and is contrary to the goals of any sports program. It is encouraging to note that newly developed methods for hormone detection by urine analysis are currently in use in Europe and will soon be widely utilized in international competition. These methods may help bring this dangerous form of "doping" under effective control.

Losing Weight

The basic principles of energy balance applicable to weight gain also govern weight loss. The elimination of one pound of body fat requires the expenditure of approximately 3500 Calories more than are consumed. 3500 Calories can represent the total daily caloric intake of an active young man. With this amount he will utilize the energy stored in only one pound of body fat, if he pursues his normal daily activities and eats nothing for an entire 24-hour period. (Anyone attempting this brief period of starvation will note weight loss somewhat greater than one pound because of the water excreted with the metabolic waste products of fat and protein.)

Who Should Lose Weight?   Skin-fold measurements of high school and college athletes, taken as part of their pre-competition physical examinations, have revealed an excessively high level of fatness. It is well known that body fat levels for both men and women increase with age, and that obesity is a widespread problem among the adult population in the United States. It has become common to find undesirable levels of fatness among a large proportion of high school and college football and basketball players, swimmers, crew members, field hockey players, etc.

The skin-fold measurements of high school boys have indicated levels of body fat averaging 15 to 18 per cent of body weight. A level of 8 to 10 per cent would probably be a better upper limit for a male in his late teens. It would make sense therefore for a large number of American athletes to reduce, to improve their general fitness and most particularly their athletic performance.

It is advisable to measure skin fat folds at the beginning of any weight reduction program. Estimating the amount of body fat allows one to individualize a weight loss schedule. The individual's schedule should take into account sex, age, athletic activity, and also the present and desired fat percentages.

Weight reduction programs are often requested by 12- to 14-year-old girls who wish to participate in gymnastics, figure skating, or other sports. This particular group warrants unusual care. Some girls with relatively large skeletal frames are apt to seek weight levels which are completely unrealistic.

Their excess weight loss will have to come from reduction in muscle mass, which will actually compromise their athletic performance. There is a similar danger for athletes in weight-controlled sports like wrestling, light-weight crew, and boxing, where it is too often assumed that a participant will be most effective in the lightest weight class he can possibly reach. (Methods of calculating body fatness and standards of skinfold thickness are in Appendix D.)

Planning a Weight Reduction Program. A successful weight-loss program for an active athlete must involve: (1) a realistic time schedule; (2) an appropriate training program; and (3) a diet which limits caloric intake, yet provides sufficient energy to allow effective participation in training and other daily activities.

Circumstances will often dictate the rate at which weight loss can be programmed, but four pounds per week would ordinarily represent the maximum healthy rate. A loss of no more than two pounds per week is usually better. Remembering that each pound of lost fat requires a deficit of 3500 Calories, it is simple arithmetic to calculate the necessary combination of exercise and dieting required. It is often helpful to plot a simple graph, showing the anticipated weight at each stage of a constant-rate weight reduction program. (There are examples in Appendix C.)

The energy expenditure tables for various forms of exercise often discourage the would-be dieter. He or she may lose interest upon learning that it will take seven hours of bicycle-riding to expend the energy equivalent to one pound of body fat. But when viewed in the context of two one-half-hour bicycle rides each day, representing a lost pound of fat each week, 12 pounds in three months, the program becomes more appealing.

Such a program was set up recently for a promising young figure-skater, in the form of a half-hour bike ride each way to and from her daily workouts. At the same time, she reduced her daily intake by 500 Calories, to a level of 1800 Calories, creating a diet deficit of 3500 Calories each week—the equivalent of one pound of fat. With the additional energy expenditure of the two one-half-hour bike rides added to the modest diet reduction, she had a caloric deficit equivalent to two pounds of fat loss per week. In little more than a month she lost ten pounds.

Attempting to create a caloric deficit through diet alone, or through exercise programs alone, is usually unsuccessful. A reduction of 6000 to 8000 Calories per week below customary intakes would essentially be a starvation diet, and few people could stay on it for long. On such minimal intakes daily academic and training demands could not be met. Similarly, an exercise increase equivalent to 6000–8000 Calories, without added food, would be physically impossible for most people.

Therefore, maintaining (or working towards) a high level of exercise is an essential component of any weight reduction program. Substantial exercise allows one to live with a caloric deficit and still get enough food to prevent the weakness and fatigue which can ruin an effective training program. *Most active athletes need at least 2000 Calories per day;* and with appropriate physical activity, a 2000-Calorie diet can result in significant weight loss.

It is clear that the larger the dietary intake, the easier it is to include adequate amounts of all essential nutrients in the daily diet. As pointed out earlier, however, a Basic Diet containing no more than 1200 to 1400 Calories can provide all needed nutrients, if the food is well selected (most simply from the Four Food Groups). When the diet is increased to 2000 Calories, there is obviously more latitude for meeting nutritional needs, and for selecting some preferred foods. If the diet is well planned to insure effective caloric intake throughout the day, it will provide ample energy for academic activities, as well as for the demands of training and competition.

A 2000-Calorie Reducing Diet.   A 2000-Calorie diet is presented below. Diets similar to this have been successfully used by athletes for weight reduction in several programs (and variant low-calorie diets can be found in the Appendix). The diet is planned around three conventional meals, but there is also an alternate form, preferred by many not living at home or eating at training tables, which is based on snacks throughout the day and one large meal in the evening.

Weight reduction diets too often neglect the noon or early afternoon meal. Midday food intake is extremely important in providing the energy for afternoon training activities. In this 2000-Calorie diet, the Four Food Groups are appropriately represented and all the essential nutrients are provided in amounts adequate for even the most active athlete. There is no need for supplements (with the possible exception of iron supplementation for some girls, particularly those with unusually large menstrual losses).

Foods to be avoided are those with high caloric density, such as fats, nuts, cheeses, dairy products, and fatty meats. (Luncheon meats, sausages, and frankfurters are high in fat content and in caloric density.) Foods that can be eaten liberally for main meals or snacks are those with low caloric density but some satiety value, like vegetables with high cellulose content and fruits with a reasonable amount of bulk. Milk should be skimmed and soft drinks sugar-free.

Dieting is a good time to develop a healthy water-drinking habit, since drinking water can compensate for some of the deprived feeling that comes from eating less. Alcoholic beverages have a high caloric density and should be avoided.

The importance of a reasonable time period for weight loss cannot be overemphasized. However, time is sometimes not available. The football player reducing for wrestling competition after the football season may wish to lose 15 to 20 pounds in four or five weeks. His conditioning and weight reduction program must be very carefully supervised; and strict adherence to a well-planned diet is essential. A four- to five-week period should be the minimal length of time for losing this amount of weight; anything shorter would be incompatible with either good health or effective athletic performance. *No healthy reduction program calls for weight loss at a rate in excess of four pounds a week.* (See Chapter 9 with respect to weight-controlled sports.)

2,000 CALORIE REDUCING DIET

Breakfast

½   cup orange juice
1   soft-boiled egg
1   slice whole wheat toast
2   teasp. margarine
1   glass skim milk or other
      beverage

Total Calories: 345

Snack

1   banana

Total Calories: 100

Lunch

      hamburger (3 oz.) on a
         roll with relish
½   sliced tomato
1   glass skim milk
1   medium apple

Total Calories: 510

Snack

1   carton fruit-flavored
      yogurt
1   cup grape juice

Total Calories: 385

Dinner

      baked chicken marengo
         (½ breast)
¾   cup rice
5-6   Brussel sprouts
      green salad with French
         dressing
1   small piece gingerbread
1   cup skim milk or other
      beverage

Total Calories: 660

Daily Total Calories: 2000

We had a challenging problem recently in our Sports Medicine Nutrition Clinic, when three members of the varsity crew came in for counseling. They appeared early in March, weighing between 170 and 175 pounds, and wanted to reduce to 158 pounds to qualify for competition in the light-weight crew. They were over six feet tall and had been in intensive crew training since the beginning of the academic year. From the middle of January on, their workouts had increased in intensity.

Measurements of skin fat folds showed that 16 to 18 per cent of their total body weight consisted of fat (and that such losses could come from fat, without reduction of lean tissue). The first race and weigh-in was only four weeks away. The reduction of 12 to 17 pounds in a four-week period, four pounds per week, represented the maximum compatible with good health. The fact that they all ate at a training table was helpful, since it made it easier to stick to a prescribed dietary regimen.

Each was given a specific 2000-Calorie diet and urged to increase his training activity to a total energy expenditure of 4500 Calories per day. They were to record all food intake for the four-week period, weigh themselves only once each week, and report to the Clinic for diet review and weigh-in at weekly intervals. Dedicated and disciplined, they were able to keep on their diets, even with their rigorous program of two-a-day workouts. They all achieved their weight goals in ample time for the first competition. By the end of the reducing period they had lowered their levels of body fat to an estimated 10 per cent. Once there, they had no trouble maintaining their desired weights throughout the season; and they were able to resume generous diets because of their high energy-expending workouts.

Somewhat later a fellow crew member attempted to lose more than a pound per day, in order to row in the light-weight boat. He reduced his eating to a starvation level. After about 10 days, he acquired a febrile viral illness, became anemic, and had to be dropped from competition. The moral was clear: alterations in body weight cannot be safely and effectively achieved without adequate advance planning.

SUMMARY

This chapter has considered the body's need for energy, and how energy is provided by food. Food and body energy are measured as heat and expressed as calories. One gram of fat provides 9 Calories; a gram of either protein or carbohydrate provides 4 Calories; and a gram of alcohol provides 7 Calories.

Energy is required to meet the needs of physical work and exercise, for maintaining body temperature, and for the essential metabolic functions of the body. Basal energy expenditures, or "basal metabolism," is influenced by body size, degree of fatness, and age. Large, young, lean individuals, especially those who are growing, have the highest rates of basal metabolism.

The athlete who desires to gain weight must take in more calories than he expends. In the case of a very large and active athlete this may require an enormous amount of food. In all instances the food should not be high in animal fat. Individuals with family histories of early cardiovascular disease should not attempt to gain weight without medical consultation.

Specific training and conditioning programs should accompany the high caloric intake, if muscle and not fat is to be the major tissue component of added weight. The athlete must know which foods most efficiently contribute calories, since the most common reason for failure to gain weight is lack of appreciation of the amount of food needed. In addition, it is often difficult for the active young athlete to find time to prepare and eat a diet of sufficient size. This is a real problem, and adequate time must be set aside. Gaining at a rate of approximately two pounds per week is generally the recommended maximum.

The use of testosterone or other anabolic steroids such as Dianobol has no place in any athletic program. They are unethical, of questionable use in improving performance, and there is no doubt that they contribute to diminished testicular function and can permanently damage reproductive tissues. If used before growth is complete, they can stunt growth.

Weight reducing requires an expenditure of energy in excess of intake, approximately 3500 Calories for each pound of body fat. Weight reduction should be carefully calculated and planned. In general, the schedule should not call for the loss of more than 2-4 pounds per week, and it should be based on a daily caloric intake of no less than 2000 Calories for an average male athlete. Weight loss accompanied by sufficient exercise and an adequate diet will cause loss of body fat. Weight loss without exercise, relying on starvation, will result in a wasting of muscle tissue.

SUGGESTED READINGS AND REFERENCE WORKS

1. Astrand, P. and Rodahl, K.: *Textbook of Work Physiology,* Chapter 2., McGraw-Hill Book Co., New York, 1970.

2. Willams, M.H.: *Drugs and Athletic Performance,* Chapter 4, p. 87. Charles C. Thomas, Springfield, Ill., 1974.

3. Bullen, B.A., Reed, R.B., and Mayer, J.: "Physical Activity of Obese and Nonobese Adolescent Girls." *Am. J. Clin. Nutr.* 14:211, 1964.

4. "The Way to a Man's Heart." American Heart Association, New York, N.Y.

5. "Planning Fat-Controlled Meals." American Heart Association, New York, N.Y.

6. Frasier, A.D.: "Androgens and Athletes." *Am. J. Dis. of Child.,* 125:479, 1973.

five

THE ENERGY DEMANDS OF THE ATHLETE

The biochemical reactions with which food produces energy for exercise are complex, but in recent years research has added substantially to our knowledge of how diet can aid athletic performance. Until recently, accepted nutrition dogma held that all athletes perform at their best on a "well-balanced" diet. However, improved understanding of energy metabolism has disclosed that different types of activity depend on different energy-producing systems. And considerable evidence suggests that what is appropriate food intake for one sport may not support optimal performance for another.

That being the case, this chapter discusses the energy pathways, how they are used to meet the distinct needs of various kinds of exercise, and what particular dietary modifications can be made to satisfy these needs.

THE SOURCES OF ENERGY

In one sense, the body is an energy-transformer, taking in fuel and converting it to energy to build or replace its parts and to keep it mobile. This last function, actually physical exercise, requires the conversion of chemical energy into mechanical energy for muscle movement. In order to do this, the body relies on certain internal sources, which ones depending on a number of variables: how quickly the energy is needed, how strenuously the muscles must work, and how long the activity lasts. In the case of the athlete, another factor becomes extremely important—his capacity to introduce oxygen into his bloodstream and deliver it to body tissues, particularly working muscles. This has a significant influence on which energy system his body will primarily utilize, and its effect will be more clearly understood as the chapter develops.

In approaching the energy sources, keep in mind that the biochemical reactions which take place in the body are part of an intricate network of interlocking energy cycles. We are not certain about the precise nature of these cycles and how they interact. But we do know some simple facts: Energy production is *not* linear. The body does not switch in and out of sequential energy systems, permanently turning off one source as it moves on to the next. There occurs rather a smooth phasing with overlapping from one energy source into another, as the energy demands increase during any given athletic event.

For the purposes of explanation, however, it is helpful to divide the energy sources into three separate categories.

The ATP-PC System

The immediate source of energy for muscle work is a compound called "ATP" (adenosine triphosphate), which is formed in the muscles by the metabolism of carbohydrates, fats, and, to an almost insignificant degree, proteins. In plain terms, ATP is the ultimate fuel which all muscle cells need in order to do their work. It can be rapidly metabolized to meet the needs of sudden outbursts of activity in intensive, short-term exercise, such as shot putting, pole vaulting, or track and swimming sprints.

Since the body is able to metabolize ATP without the need for oxygen, the reaction is classified as "anaerobic" (occuring in the *absence* of oxygen). This is important in strenuous exercise, where the heart and lungs cannot deliver oxygen quickly enough to the muscles. Under such circumstances it is easy to see why a dashman, for instance, who may not even take a breath during a 50-yard dash, would basically depend on an anaerobic energy supply.

If the energy demands last for more than brief spurts, the muscle cells contain a high-energy back-up compound, phosphocreatine, or "PC," which can almost instantaneously provide the energy required to regenerate ATP. But within a matter of minutes of vigorous exercise the small stores of ATP-PC are used up. And the body must turn to a second line of energy supply in order to recharge the ATP-PC system.

Glycogen

The second energy source is "glycogen," a storage carbohydrate found only in animal tissues, which the body makes from glucose (a simple sugar) and stores in limited amounts in the liver and muscles. When ATP-PC energy has been exhausted through exercise, glycogen can be metabolized within the muscle cells to restore ATP. Again, this metabolism is primarily carried out in the absence of oxygen, so it is also designed as anaerobic.

As will be shown, a well-designed nutrition program can supplement proper conditioning to insure maximum glycogen storage. This is very important for athletes like middle-distance runners, since glycogen is a major source of energy for heavy exertion lasting more than a few minutes. It may have even more impact in long-distance events, where endurance appears to be measurably improved when competitors' muscles are "loaded" with maximal stores of glycogen.

Fats and Carbohydrates

As continuing exercise progressively depletes the stores of ATP-PC and muscle glycogen, the body increasingly resorts to a third source of energy. This last fuel comes from the "aerobic" (occuring in the *presence* of oxygen) metabolism of carbohydrates (more specifically, glucose) and fats.

Although fats can be stored in body depots in virtually inexhaustible supplies, their slower rate of metabolism makes

[1]Body stores of protein make only a minimal contribution to energy production, as long as fat deposits are available.

them a less efficient source of quick energy, particularly for the casual athlete. This is not necessarily true for the highly conditioned competitor, and a prime object of conditioning is to improve oxygen-burning capacity. With intensive training the athlete can appreciably increase his or her efficiency in utilizing fat as an energy source. This is especially helpful to endurance events. It means, quite simply, that one can delay the glycogen depletion by burning fat instead. This is called "glycogen-sparing," and it appears to enhance endurance performance significantly. In the context of the strenuous exercise demanded by intensive competition, glucose metabolism makes a relatively minor contribution. The figure on p. 78 gives a graphic outline of the energy sources for various athletic events.

THE IMPORTANCE OF
TRAINING AND DIET

The figure shows the sources of energy and when they are needed to meet the demands of muscle work in a wide range of athletic events. But one must remember that the anaerobic and aerobic systems are not entirely distinct. In order to regenerate the anaerobic system (ATP-PC and glycogen), oxygen must be utilized eventually to build up the chains of energy reactions leading to ATP. For that reason general conditioning programs are crucial to maximize oxygen utilization capacity, even when training for events where the exertion must be largely explosive. (The additional significance of specific muscle group training will be discussed later in the chapter.)

Of course innate ability and mental attitudes cannot be forgotten. Together with training and conditioning, they are the determinants of champions. And there is still another factor which can provide the decisive edge, one which we are concerned with particularly: dietary management tailored to the specific needs of muscle work.

Any dietary recommendation must be considered in the light of two important qualifications: First, all nutritional

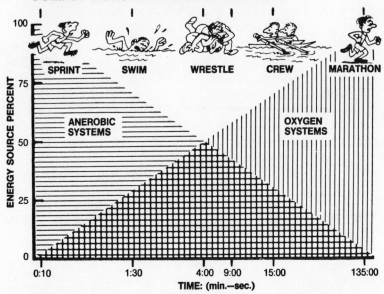

PRINCIPAL ENERGY MECHANISMS IN
COMPETITIONS OF VARYING DURATION

See Fox, E. L., The Physiologic Basis of Physical Education and Athletics. W. B. Saunders Co., Philadelphia.

planning should take into account the individual athlete's food preferences and cultural eating patterns. The nutrition-related goals can be reached through a variety of routes; and wide freedom of choice can be a significant part of the psychological preparation for competition. Second, it must be emphasized that the response to dietary preparation will vary among different individuals, when they are getting ready for intense competition. The High Performance Diet (which follows) provides a good example.

DIET MANAGEMENT FOR ALL-OUT EFFORT OF SHORT DURATION

Getting ready for the short-term contest requires two preparatory steps: (1) Adequate nutritional intake during the days prior to the competition and (2) measures to ensure that muscle sources of ATP-PC and glycogen have not been exhausted by muscular work immediately before the actual event. During track and swimming meets for example, where competitors are often involved in several daily events, time should be allotted between contests for replenishing optimal levels of glycogen and ATP-PC. Such periods will also allow time to clear the muscles of the by-products of anaerobic metabolism, such as lactic acid. Energy depletion and the accumulation of lactic acid both contribute to fatigue.

Throughout the day of the meet, the competitors in short-term events will have particular need for an adequate supply of carbohydrate and water. Successful athletes have often met these needs by limiting food intake on the day of competition to frequent but modest drinks of fruit juices or water. (A small amount of additional sugar can be added to them, if the individual can tolerate such concentrations of sugar.) Hard candies and water are preferred by some athletes, while complete liquid meals, which will be described later, are becoming increasingly popular with others.

Many athletes value a feeling of lightness, particularly as they enter major competition. This can be enhanced by a pre-competition diet that restricts foods of high residue, minimizing the amount of food which remains in the stomach. Foods high in fat, in particular, should be limited on the day of competition; they leave the stomach slowly and may contribute to a persistent feeling of fullness. Depending on the individual, it may be helpful to limit intakes of the following during the days immediately preceding important competition: raw fruits and vegetables, dried fruits, nuts, whole-grain cereal products, berry and fruit pies, milk, and cheese. (See Chapter 8 for more information about pre-event meals.)

MEETING THE ENERGY NEEDS
FOR INTERMEDIATE LENGTH EVENTS

The High-Performance Diet

A variety of athletic contests demand intense muscle exertion for periods of from 4–5 up to 10 minutes and longer. The mile run, the wrestling match, the middle-distance swimming events, and rowing contests all demand truly maximal exertion without rest. After two or three minutes (very roughly speaking), the anaerobic energy available through ATP and PC is exhausted. And in these events, even the most highly-conditioned athlete cannot provide enough oxygen to his muscles to supply the needed energy through aerobic metabolism alone. The other potential source is stored glycogen; performance may be significantly upgraded by increasing muscle glycogen stores to support an increase of anaerobic energy production.

In recent years it has been found that glycogen stores can be greatly increased when a high-carbohydrate regimen is introduced during the week preceding competition, and increasing numbers of athletes are utilizing this glycogen-loading "High Performance Diet" to provide optimal energy. For many, but not all, it has proven successful in improving performance in the mid-length contests mentioned above, and also in the long-term events, like the marathon and cross-country skiing.

The physiologic basis of what is called here a "High Performance Diet" was developed in this country from studies by a team of Swedish physiologists. They observed that on a normal diet the average concentration of glycogen in the muscle tissues was approximately 1.75 grams per 100 grams of muscle. After three days of a diet limited to fat and protein (with carbohydrate entirely eliminated), the glycogen level fell to 0.6 grams per 100 grams of muscle. When the diet was then reversed, with large amounts of carbohydrates added, the level increased to 3.5 grams. And it was further shown that if one depleted the glycogen level by strenuous exercise of a specific muscle while on the low-carbohydrate diet, and then switched to a high-carbohydrate diet, the glycogen level rose to as high as 4.7 grams in the exercised muscle.

In short, this study demonstrated that glycogen levels could be almost tripled through diet manipulation and a related program of first exhausting then replenishing muscle glycogen stores. On the basis of these findings, the High Performance Diet was developed.

Assuming a six-day period of preparation, the High Performance Diet is initiated (Phase I) on the Sunday or Monday prior to a Saturday contest. For the first two and one-half days, the diet consists mainly of proteins and fats. The essential feature of the diet (as prescribed in our Clinic) is the limitation of daily carbohydrate intake to approximately 100 grams, or 400 Calories. This period of restricted carbohydrate intake must accompany a vigorous training schedule, exercising the specific muscles to be involved in the competition in order to deplete their glycogen stores.

By Wednesday most athletes find that they tire easily in their workouts. Because of the glycogen depletion, they experience unusual fatigue and compromised performance during workouts. These adverse effects on training must be recognized as the inevitable results of the low-carbohydrate phase of the diet, and taken into account in judging the limitations and advantages of this regimen.

Beginning with dinner on the third day, the athlete switches to a diet high in carbohydrate (Phase II). The diet still contains adequate protein and fat, but also unrestricted amounts of carbohydrate. The only limitation in this phase of the diet is the general restriction on both salty and high-residue foods. (See Chapter 6.)

The high-carbohydrate, low-salt, low-residue diet is then maintained until the day of competition. During this stage we have found that a portion of the necessary high-carbohydrate intake can be effectively provided by fruit-flavored drinks rich in glucose. These provide a high concentration of readily available carbohydrate, without the detrimental residues of bulky foods. Commercially available through pharmacies* and reasonably palatable, they can be taken as a supplement to the Phase II diet, up to and even during the day of competition. They should contribute 1000 to 1500

*Such products as Poly-cose® (Ross Laboratories) and Cal-power® (General Mills).

THE HIGH PERFORMANCE DIET

FOOD GROUPS & DAILY AMOUNTS

	Phase I		Phase II	
Meat	20-25	ounces	8	ounces
Breads & Cereals	4	servings	10-16	servings
Vegetables	3-4	servings	3-4	servings
Fruit	4	servings	10	servings
Fats	8-9	ounces	4-6	ounces
Desserts	1-2	servings (only fruits & unsweetened gelatins)	2	servings (include ice cream, cookies, etc.)
Beverages	Unlimited (no sugar)		Unlimited (assuming proper calorie control)	

SAMPLE MEAL PLANS

PHASE I	PHASE II

Breakfast

8	oz. unsweet-ened orange juice	8	oz. orange juice (O.K. sweetened)
4	eggs	1	egg
1	slice toast	2	slices toast
4	tsp. butter or margarine	2	tsp. butter or margarine
4	strips bacon	1	cup cereal

Lunch

1	meat sandwich (with butter or margarine & mayonnaise)	2	sandwiches— each with 1 oz. meat or cheese, ½ tsp butter or margarine

2-3 cheese sticks
 1   tossed salad
     with oil
     dressing
 1   medium apple
     or orange

8   oz. low-fat
    milk

2   large bananas

Snack(s)

 2   meat sandwiches
     (with butter
     or margarine)
 1   cheese stick
 1   medium apple
     or banana

2   sandwiches—
    meat or non-
    meat
1   serving fruit
8   oz. low-fat
    milk

Dinner

10   oz. meat
     (not ham)
 1   small baked
     potato, with
     2-3 tsp.
     butter or
     marg. and
     1 tblsp. sour
     cream
 1   serving veg-
     etable (no
     corn, etc.)
     with 1-2 tsp.
     butter or
     margarine
 1   tossed salad

 1   small apple
     D'Zerta

4   oz. meat
    (not ham)
1   medium baked
    potato, with
    1 tsp.
    butter, etc.

1   serving
    vegetable

2   rolls, with
    1 tsp. butter
    or margarine
2   servings fruit
2   servings
    beverage,
    such as
    Hy-Cal® or
    Cal-power®

Calories of carbohydrate, which will be utilized to build up the stores of muscle glycogen. These caloric needs can also be met (less expensively by a daily quart of Kool-aid and a bag of jelly beans or raisins.

The High Performance Diet requires considerable insight and dedication on the part of the participant. The most demanding aspect for most individuals is the first phase, with its restricted carbohydrate intake during a period of intensive training. Less demanding is the high-carbohydrate, low-residue diet later in the week.

For most athletes, it is advisable to limit the High Performance Diet to important competitions. For more casual contests, a limited version can be followed, simply utilizing Phase II, the high-carbohydrate intake late in the week. This modification will be more desirable for those athletes who don't wish to compromise the effectiveness of their training on Tuesday or Wednesday.

DIETARY CONSIDERATIONS
FOR ENDURANCE CONTESTS

The High Performance Diet seems particularly helpful when intensive output is required for more than ten or fifteen minutes without rest. When competition is at hand, of course, other considerations should affect the choice of diet.

On the morning of competition, athletes should avoid high bulk and fatty foods like pancakes, fried eggs, bacon and sausages, choosing instead such carbohydrate sources as toast or muffins with jam or honey. Lightly sweetened fruit juices throughout the day are popular, and they are particularly helpful for maintenance of fluid intake. (Their carbohydrate content helps prevent hunger, but contributes only minimally to energy needs.)

In preparing for a lengthy afternoon competition, the athlete will usually require a light lunch of low-residue, non-fatty foods taken at least two and one-half hours prior to the contest. Within the indicated limits, the athlete should eat those foods he likes and which he feels contribute to his best performance. The preferred foods should always take precedence; one should never deprive an athlete of the foods that he thinks will make him win.

Some care must be taken in choosing high-carbohydrate foods during the day of competition. If carbohydrate is taken in too concentrated a form—as in undiluted honey, glucose tablets or syrups—it can cause a pooling of large amounts of water in the upper gastrointestinal tract, with resulting discomfort and diarrhea. The tense, nervous athlete is apt to have a poorly functioning stomach anyway, and may be particularly vulnerable to high concentrations of carbohydrate.

Diluted sweetened fruit juices, or fruit-flavored non-carbonated drinks are best tolerated with no more than a 10 to 15 per cent concentration of carbohydrate. Honey-sweetened tea may produce undesirable side effects in the very young athlete who is not accustomed to drinking caffeine-containing beverages; in particular the stimulation from caffeine can be followed by depression.

Salt and water needs are dealt with in Chapter 6. Suffice it to say here that the salt needs of even a marathon runner competing in warm weather rarely exceed the amount obtained from a normal diet. Too much salt compromises hydration and may contribute to heat-related disease. The problem is exaggerated by salt tablets. Maintaining hydration and avoiding excessive increase in body temperature are of far more concern than any threat of salt depletion. The water requirements for long competition demand constant attention, particularly in a warm climate, with an hourly intake of water beforehand and continued intake at appropriate intervals throughout the event.

LIQUID MEALS

There are a number of products which have been recently developed for hospital patients unable to take solid foods.[2]

[2]Examples are "Ensure"® (Ross Laboratories), "SustaCal,"® and Sustagen® (Mead Johnson Laboratories). Each comes in 8 oz. cans which can easily be transported and chilled; and each is available in several flavors.

Highly concentrated calorically and of high quality, they have also been used successfully in sports programs for pre-game meals and as a source of energy and hydration during day-long competition. (These liquid meals should not be confused with instant powdered meals or meal supplements, "instant breakfasts," etc., which are customarily mixed with milk. Such mixtures have fat, protein, and electrolyte concentrations which may be too great for use before athletic contests.)

For those who find them palatable and satisfying, the liquid meals have several advantages. They leave the stomach very rapidly, with essentially no residue, because they are completely absorbed from the gastrointestinal tract. Their fluid and caloric contributions are significant and highly desirable. But despite the absence of uncomfortable feelings of fullness, they contribute a feeling of satiety.

Day-long competition—common in swimming meets, track meets, and tennis tournaments—has traditionally presented difficult food-planning problems. Too often athletes have had no interest in food, and their performance has suffered, notably toward the end of the day. The energy and satiety provided by sipping chilled cans of the liquid meals intermittently during the day can offer the nutritional answer for many. (See Chapter 9 for more about liquid meals.)

A WORD OF WARNING

Do not introduce new dietary plans or new foods shortly before an important competition: You may be inviting a last-minute encounter with an unexpected food intolerance.

The athlete should do his experimenting early in the season, not when preparing for important events, and this is particularly true of the High Performance Diet. Some competitors discover that they can be most effective if they skip Phase I, the low-carbohydrate diet early in the week, and limit their special diet preparation to a modest increase in carbohydrate intake toward the end of the week. Others may derive a worthwhile advantage from following the diet plan closely for the entire week. Any foods planned for the day of competition should certainly be investigated long beforehand. On that day especially, the tense and sensitive gastrointestinal tract should not be challenged by new and strange foods.

SUMMARY

In preparation for important competition the athlete's diet should assure the following: adequate fluid intake, avoidance of undue water retention (particularly from salty foods), minimal food residues, and an optimal supply of energy.

Specific energy demands differ, depending on the immediacy of the need, the intensity of the muscle work, and the duration of the event. Dietary management can be adjusted to meet the demands of the particular competition.

The short-term, all-out effort (roughly, of less than two or three minutes duration) will depend primarily on the anaerobic metabolism of ATP-PC stores in the muscle cells. The principal considerations for these events are good hydration, an adequate diet, and rest between contests, to build up ATP-PC stores and to get rid of the by-products of anaerobic metabolism.

An important energy source for intermediate-length competition (relatively intense events lasting from approximately three to ten minutes) comes from the anaerobic metabolism of glycogen stores in the muscles. The High Performance Diet, a regimen for the week prior to such a contest, is designed to provide maximum stores of glycogen.

All energy sources will be mobilized to meet the needs of prolonged effort in the endurance contest. Again, the High Performance Diet may be effective. It will supply large stores of muscle glycogen, for an early advantage in the event, and for a large source of anaerobic energy for events of long duration.

It is important to caution that the High Performance Diet is not equally beneficial to all athletes. It should be undertaken only after experimentation early in the training season, so each athlete will be familiar with his or her reactions to it.

During day-long meets conventional foods may not be well tolerated. Liquid meals satisfy an athlete's needs for satiety and a sense of well-being, without compromising hydration or the sense of fitness.

SUGGESTED READINGS AND REFERENCE WORKS

1. Mathews, D.K., and Fox, E.L.: *Physiologic Basis of Physical Education and Athletics.* W.B. Saunders, Phila. Pa., 1971.

2. Bergstrom, J. and Huetrnan, E.: "Nutrition for Maximal Sports Performance (Glycogen loading)." *J.A.M.A.*, 221:991, 1972.

3. Consolazio, C.F., and Johnson, H.L.: "Dietary Carbohydrate and Work Capacity."*Am. J. Clin. Nutr.,* 25:85, 1972.

4. Lewis, S., and Gutin, B.: "Nutrition and Endurance." *Am. J. Clin. Nutrit.,* 26:10,11, 1973.

5. Astrand, P.: "Something Old—Something New (Glycogen loading)." *Nutrition Today,* 3:9, 1968.

six

THE ATHLETE'S NEED FOR WATER AND SALT

Obviously, no one "essential" nutrient can be more essential than any other. But the constant need for water makes it particularly important from the standpoint of time. Most essential nutrients may be absent from the diet for periods of several weeks to months without serious deficiency symptoms. Not so with water. It must be regularly available, for without it we cannot survive for more than a few days.

THE IMPORTANCE OF ADEQUATE HYDRATION

Body water serves many vital functions. Nutrients, hormones, waste products, and antibodies are all transported in the water of blood plasma to the water which surrounds individual cells. All of the body's important chemical reactions are carried out in water and are significantly less efficient when an adequate amount of body water is not available.

The role of water in regulating body temperature is of particular importance to the athlete. The excessive heat generated by exercise must be dissipated—and the most effective way is through the evaporation of sweat. This mechanism fails to function effectively, however, if the water supply is inadequate to meet the needs of the sweat glands. (Loss of body heat by sweat evaporation will also be hampered if the body is too completely covered or if the environmental humidity is too great to allow effective evaporation.)

The critical importance of adequate hydration, particularly for high energy output and endurance activities, was clearly demonstrated in the early attempts to climb Mount Everest. An unsuccessful effort by a Swiss team was attributed to their short supply of fuel, only sufficient to melt snow for one daily pint of water per man during the last three days of the ascent. As the climbers became dehydrated, severe fatigue developed and they had to turn back. Sir Edmund Hilary later succeeded with his party, as they carried sufficient fuel to provide each man with a water allotment of seven pints per day. This was not an excessive amount, considering the tremendous energy required for the last stages of the climb, and the very low humidity at high altitudes.

THE DISTRIBUTION AND REGULATION OF BODY WATER

Roughly 60 per cent of adult male body weight is comprised of water. Females have somewhat less, because of their larger percentage of fat tissue, which has less water content. To function effectively, water must be specifically distributed in the body: approximately 35 per cent within cells as intracellular water, approximately 25 per cent between cells as extracellular water, and the remainder (approximately 40 per cent) in the circulating blood. If the distribution within and outside of body cells is significantly disturbed, energy metabolism will be compromised, whether or not the total amount of body water is normal.

Daily losses of body water are relatively large, even under circumstances of moderate temperature and light physical activity. The entire mass of water (again, approximately 60 per cent of adult weight) must be replaced every 11 to 13 days. Vigorous exercise, or high temperatures and low humidity, will further increase the need for water. A normal adult in an average environment requires approximately 2.5 liters of water every day (a little more than 2.5 quarts). This water comes from the water in food, as well as from drinking water and other beverages. In addition, water is formed when food is metabolized for energy. (Fats, carbohydrates, and protein are all metabolized to carbon dioxide and water.) This so-called metabolic water usually accounts for approximately one-fifth of an average day's total water requirement.

Under normal circumstances, the single largest outlet for water loss is through the urine. When large amounts of protein are taken in the diet and metabolized, the resulting nitrogenous waste products are excreted by the kidney. When intakes of minerals and electrolytes are in excess of the body's needs, they too are excreted, and cause an additional loss of body water in the urine.

Water losses occur not only from the skin and through the kidneys but also from the surface of the lungs. Inspired air picks up moisture as it contacts lung surfaces, and upon expiration discharges it to the external environment. Moisture loss from the skin through sweating is often obvious during exercise, but there is also a constant loss of water which is not obvious, from the normally moist skin to the less moist air. The losses of water through breathing and from the skin (without obvious sweating) are referred to as "insensible" water losses. The lower the level of humidity in the environment, and the more rapidly air is moving over the skin and lungs, the greater the insensible water loss will be.

Air travel by athletes has substantially increased in recent years. The very dry air of airplanes, combined with the rapid circulation of air in airplane ventilation, cause large insensible losses of water. In a recent case team members taking a three and one-half hour flight in a standard commercial jet liner were found to have lost as much as two pounds, more than a full quart of body water each. Such water losses should be compensated for by increased drinking prior to and during the flight or be promptly replaced afterward.

The insensible water loss from long airplane flights can contribute to so-called "jet-lag." To counteract the effects, bottles of water should be provided for a team on long flights; and care should be taken to avoid dehydrating beverages containing caffeine and alcohol. Fruit juices and soft drinks without caffeine are often served, but usually not in sufficient amounts to correct the insensible water loss of a long journey. The miniscule paper cups and reluctant water spigots of the average jet liner are of little help.

Regulation of body water through the rate of urinary excretion is obvious to everyone. The volume differs greatly from hour to hour, in keeping with the variances in water intake and other water losses. In stabilizing body water, the volume control of urine production is the single most important mechanism. But there are definite limitations on the efficiency of the kidneys in controlling water balance when there are prolonged water deficits or striking excesses of water intake.

What is much less widely appreciated is that thirst is not a sensitive indicator of the need for additional water. An athlete preparing for a contest may be suffering from a significant lack of body water and still not be thirsty. It is particularly important that a healthy supply of water be assured during the intensely emotional periods prior to competition, most effectively by precise scheduling of fluid intake. *Don't depend on thirst to tell you when water is needed.*

THE WATER REQUIREMENTS OF THE ATHLETE

As indicated above, the lean, non-fat tissues of the body contain more water than the fat tissues. The higher water content of muscle tissue is related to its metabolic activity; more water is needed to carry out the chemical reactions involved in the vigorous functions of muscle. For this reason, water constitutes a larger percentage of the body weight of the well-conditioned athlete. The non-athlete male and the average female will have respectively close to 60 per cent and 55 per cent of their weight in body water. The more muscular male athletes, such as those participating in swimming, track, and gymnastics, have been found to have 70 per cent or more of their weight in water. Football and baseball players, with more body fat, have somewhat less water—approximately 63 per cent.

A series of dynamic changes take place in the distribution of body water during exercise and muscle work. When exercise begins, water is immediately transferred from the extracellular fluid space to the intracellular space within the cells. This transfer facilitates the production of energy. The extracellular fluid that moves into the muscle cells is rapidly replaced by water from blood plasma, thereby reducing the volume of circulating blood. The amount of blood plasma that is available to flow to the kidneys is thus reduced, and urine production is decreased. Every athlete knows that urinary volume decreases (conveniently) during a prolonged period of active exercise.

Once exercise commences—and water is lost through sweating and increased breathing—this reduced excretion of urinary water provides a control mechanism which helps to conserve body water. Mechanisms for increased water intake are not nearly as effective. Following a period of exercise and resulting dehydration the average thirst response will not in itself call for complete replacement of body water for a considerable period of time, often up to three days or more. This lag period of so-called "involuntary hypohydration" (in which water intake is inadequate to compensate for water demand) can be cumulative. As a result, after two or three days of dehydrating workouts, water deprivation can reach serious levels. Again, the need for a prescribed schedule of water intake to maintain body weight is extremely important.

The athlete who is well conditioned and acclimatized to exercise in high temperatures will voluntarily drink more often than one who is not as well trained. The acclimatized athlete will also sweat more profusely and will thus more effectively dissipate his body heat. But even the well-conditioned athlete, who drinks more, and more nearly compensates for his water losses, may spontaneously replace only one-half to one-third of his sweat losses within 24 hours of a vigorous workout in warm weather.

It is highly recommended that all athletes weigh in before and after each practice session during warm seasons or when temperatures are unseasonably high. The difference in weights before and after a practice or competition represents water loss, and the proper amount of water can be prescribed.

Numerous experiments have clearly demonstrated the benefits of adequate supplies of water. The effects are particularly apparent in high temperatures and in high humidities. The performance of most men and women will measurably deteriorate when the loss of body water reaches a level of approximately 3 per cent, or four and one-half pounds for a 150-pound person. Individuals in excellent physical condition can perform adequately until body water equal to 4 or 5 per cent of body weight is lost. Again, since the sensation of thirst is an inadequate measure of water needs, scheduled water intake is the only means of assuring adequate hydration and optimum performance.

THE ATHLETE'S NEED FOR SALT

The chemical balance of the body is partially controlled by a group of essential metallic ions that combine to provide the alkalinity (fixed-base) of body fluids. These ions, which must be supplied by the diet, include sodium, potassium, calcium, and magnesium. Sodium and potassium are in the highest concentration in body fluid. Sodium is concentrated predominantly in the extracellular fluid outside of body cells. Potassium, on the other hand, is concentrated in the intracellular fluid within body cells. As mentioned earlier, sodium and potassium are widely distributed throughout the foods we eat, with sizable amounts of sodium in the common table salt (sodium chloride) used in flavoring and preserving foods.

In addition to their part in maintaining the proper acid-base balance of the body, these metallic ions exert a primary influence on the distribution of body water. The distribution of water in the blood, and in the intracellular and extracellular fluids, is determined by the delicate balance of osmotic pressures between the various water compartments. Water is able to move freely from one water compartment to another to equalize the pressure relationships. Without any essential change in the levels of total body water, marked changes in the distribution of water which take place between the various compartments can greatly alter body function. This is particularly true when the sodium concentration of extracellular fluids is increased through excessive intakes of sodium salts. Such intakes will cause water to move from within cells (where it is needed for metabolic processes) to the extracellular compartment, in order to dilute the excessive number of sodium ions and maintain proper osmotic pressure relationships between the compartments.

Avoiding immoderate intakes of salt is therefore critical to assure optimum availability of water where it is needed during vigorous exercise, that is, within body cells. Again, except under extreme environmental conditions, we normally get more salt than we need. This is particularly true in the contemporary American population, where, increasingly, much of our food is pre-packaged and pre-salted.

The use of salt began some 3000 years ago, when it was found to be a very effective food preservative. Prior to that time man got along without adding any extra salt to his basic diet. Even today there are primitive tribes which have never added salt to their food. Many of these non-salt-using people are physically active and perform adequately in very warm climates. It is obviously clear that humans can function without adding salt to their foods, and that the body has highly effective mechanisms for regulating its supply of salt.

These mechanisms function through the excretion of salt in the urine and in the sweat. A hormone, "aldosterone," regulates the amount of sodium excreted in the urine. Also, under the influence of this hormone, the sweat glands participate by reducing the concentration of sodium ions in sweat when water losses through sweating are high.

In other words, there is salt loss as well as water loss during sweating. There is less salt in the sweat of the well-conditioned athlete, but it is difficult to tell just how much. Although the amount of water lost through sweating can be readily determined by weighing before and after exercise, there is no comparable method for determining salt loss. We do know that replacement of water in amounts equal to or somewhat in excess of that lost during exercise will improve performance. A question that obviously needs to be answered is whether or not it is necessary to promptly replace the salt that is lost.

Research has shown that when dehydration limits performance, the main cause is a decrease in the intracellular water. As described earlier, an increase in salt ions will cause an increased accumulation of extracellular water, at the expense of the metabolically active water within cells. When water is in limited supply, it should be made available for intracellular functions and not be retained between cells in the extracellular compartment.

Since any salt ingested in excess of salt losses will cause a trapping of water between cells (and deplete the intracellular water supply), it is important that water be drunk in some excess in relation to salt intake. Performance will be best if lost water is replaced with plain water. When water is not completely replaced, taking concentrated salt in the form of salt tablets can obviously be very harmful.

When is additional salt needed to replace salt lost in sweating? As was pointed out earlier, specific salt replacement is rarely needed during athletic activity, even if heavy sweat loss is involved. Americans eating a varied diet generally get more than enough sodium in their daily foods to meet even the extraordinary needs of vigorous athletic activity. But as a general guideline, if the rates of water loss exceed five to ten pounds in a given contest or workout, some consideration may be given to specific salt replacement.

This replacement is best made by adding salt to the normal diet, or it can be provided by very dilute salt-containing fluids, whose concentration should not exceed 1.5 grams of sodium chloride per liter of water (or ⅓ of a teaspoon per quart). (Commercially available salt-containing drinks taste good and have known salt concentrations. But they should not be used for all the water replacement, because they provide excessive concentrations of salt.) It is worth repeating that *taking additional salt without abundant water can be very hazardous;* and the danger is greatest when a high concentration of salt is taken, as in the form of salt tablets.

Plain water or salt-containing drinks (when appropriate) should be available in cool sanitary containers. There should be specific guidelines on how much to drink in light of measured weight losses. Since thirst alone will not prompt sufficient water intake, particularly during intense competition, hourly replacement of water losses should be scheduled.

Many of the commercial salt-containing beverages contain potassium salts as well as sodium salts. Potassium losses in sweat are negligible, under any but the most extreme conditions, and potassium depletion is not a primary concern. Nearly all potassium ingested in the average diet is quite promptly excreted in the urine, with a small amount retained for use in normal cell replacement and the repair of body tissues. Significant potassium losses can occur when the body's mechanisms for conserving potassium are disturbed by disease or the use of cathartics and diuretics. The use of the latter to reduce body weight has no place in athletics.

THE CRITICAL ROLE OF WATER IN THE PREVENTION OF HEAT DISORDERS

Life-threatening situations are fortunately rare in athletics. But nothing is more tragic than the deaths that occur each year due to heat stroke, most commonly during early-season football training. They are particularly disturbing because they are completely preventable and absolutely needless.

Modern understanding of the control of body temperature provides specific guidelines for the prevention of heat stroke. Heat stroke results from uncontrolled increases in body temperatures to levels which inhibit the regular functioning of the body's cells. The high temperatures are primarily the result of a lack of body water, which in turn compromises the basic mechanisms involved in maintaining body temperature.

The necessary loss of body heat takes place if the environmental temperature is lower than the body temperature. It almost always is, since normal body temperature is 98.6°F. As previously indicated, the major avenue of heat loss during exercise is through heat evaporation of sweat from the skin. The athlete can, through exercise, generate considerable body heat, and he needs to dissipate that heat in order to maintain normal body temperature. Sweat evaporation from the skin surfaces is the necessary cooling process.

If the humidity is too high, and sweat merely falls to the ground without evaporating, the cooling effects of evaporation are lost. Other factors can also hamper the sweat-cooling process: inadequate supply of body water for sweating; a layer of fat underneath the skin of the obese athlete, which insulates and thus helps retain body heat; or too much clothing, interfering with the evaporation of sweat.

As has been pointed out, an excess of salt in the extracellular fluid will draw water out of the cells to equalize the osmotic relationship across the cell membrane. This causes dehydration within the cells. When it reaches an advanced stage, cells cease to function; and the results are lack of energy and deterioration of athletic performance. As water leaves the blood plasma in order to dilute the salt concentrating in the extracellular fluids, there is a reduction in the circulating volume of blood. As the blood volume begins to drop, the sweating mechanism is turned off to maintain the vitally-needed circulating blood volume. If sweating and sweat evaporation are suspended for too long, there will be a dramatic rise in body temperature—often to heights in excess of 108°F. At these high temperatures, one can expect severe brain damage, heart failure, kidney failure, and death.

It is obvious that an adequate state of hydration is the first preventive measure in the avoidance of heat stroke catastrophes. It is easy to identify those who are at particular risk. They are the athletes in poor condition, who are not acclimatized to high temperatures and who are apt to be obese, with thick layers of insulating body fat. The risk is greatly increased if the athlete is exercising with a full uniform cover ing much of his skin surface.

This description most typically fits the middle lineman in the early days of late-summer football practice. His eagerness to make the team and "to get in shape" will lead him to extreme efforts; and he is apt to take faulty reassurance from the weight loss which is really dehydration. By the third or fourth day of practice, he begins his practice session having accumulated a significant deficit in body water. Further water loss limits his ability to lose body heat during practice, the sweat mechanism fails, body temperature climbs rapidly, and he is in a serious situation.

The general guidelines for prevention of heat stroke cannot be repeated too often:

1. Be concerned about the level of general conditioning before attempting exercise in hot weather.

2. Follow a well-devised plan of progressive exercise and rest while becoming acclimatized.

3. Maintain as much skin exposure as possible. In track and field events, competition without shirts can be helpful. In football, early drills in shorts and tee shirts, and later drills and competition with knit jerseys with exposed abdominal areas and no stockings, may all be advisable.

4. In early football drills, humidity and temperature may reach levels which are unsafe for any strenuous exercise. With humidity greater than 90 per cent and temperatures of 84°F. or higher, practices should be postponed.

5. All athletes should begin their practice or competition well hydrated and take care to replace fluid losses with a combination of clear water and diluted saline drinks, served at cool temperatures (50–55°F.). Any athlete

who has a persisting weight deficit of more than two or three pounds from a workout should be regarded as a high risk and excused from practice.

6. If heat stroke occurs, undress the victim and cool him with any means available: a bucket of ice water, a hose, or a cold shower. Get him to a hospital immediately. This is a true medical emergency.

Distance running in hot, humid weather can also be endangering to the health of the participant. Recognizing the need for maintenance of good levels of hydration in distance runners, the American College of Sports Medicine has recently issued the position statement on Prevention of Heat Injuries During Distance Running, which can be found in Appendix E.

SUMMARY

Maintaining a high level of physical fitness will enhance salt balance and temperature control. Avoiding excessive protein in the diet will help conserve body water in two ways: (1) by reducing obligatory urine water losses and (2) by reducing the level of metabolic heat caused by digestion of protein.

It is important for the athlete to acclimatize by training at the temperature anticipated for the event. During successive days of training or competition in a hot environment, the amount of lost body water should be measured by weighing before and after a workout or performance. A prescribed intake of water equal to, or slightly exceeding, the measured weight loss is advised. Plain water or fruit-flavored drinks are best.

If salt intake exceeds salt losses, water will be trapped between cells and the cells themselves will become dehydrated. Except in extreme circumstances, the intake of salt will be satisfied by the salt normally in the diet.

If there is doubt about the need for extra salt, don't take it. Be particularly sure not to miss meals, since the intake of fluids (like the intake of salt) is directly related to the regular intake of food. During very warm weather, meal-missing may be common, and the concerned athlete should be conscientious about eating regularly. (The salt in three meals easily replaces the salt lost with five to ten pounds of exercise-induced sweat.)

It is important to have water supplies readily available for the athlete. Intense competitors will generally ignore thirst, rather than take a short walk for a drink. The water should be cool and sanitary. There should be disposable cups and a flowing water source. (The lawn hose, water bucket, and community dipper can carry disease.) In day-long workouts or competition, the repeated drinking of small volumes of water at scheduled periods is better than a few large drinks.

Caffeine-containing beverages, such as coffee, tea, certain cola drinks, and cocoa, increase urine production and deplete the body water supply. Alcoholic beverages are even more dehydrating.

Women are generally not in the habit of drinking as regularly and as much as men, so particular attention should be paid to the fluid intake of women athletes. Again, prescribing fluid intakes at regular intervals is best.

In warm weather, in addition to weighing before and after each training session, it is important during successive days of a meet or tournament to record day-to-day weights, to be sure that fluid losses are being adequately replaced. A persistent loss of more than two or three pounds between one day and the next indicates a significant water deficit. This will compromise the performance of the athlete, and in extreme circumstances, threaten his or her safety.

SUGGESTED READINGS AND REFERENCE WORKS

1. Mathews, D.K., and Fox, E.L.: *The Physiologic Basis of Physical Education and Athletics.* Chapter 7, "Heat Balance: Prevention of Heat Stroke in Athletics." W.B. Saunders, Phila., Pa., 1971.

2. Michelsen, O.: "Nutrition and Athletics." *Food and Nutrition News,* 41:3, April, 1970.

3. Cook, D.R., Gualtiere, Wm. and Galla, S.J.: "Body Fluid Volumes of College Athletes and Non-athletes." *Med. and Sci. in Sports,* 1:217, 1969.

4. Allman, F.L.: "Heat and the Athlete." *Jour. Med. Assoc. of Georgia,* p. 282, 1967.

seven

IRON
NUTRITION

There are many reasons why iron deserves special attention. For one, an inadequate intake causes the only common nutrition deficiency recognized in this country. (While our needs for iron have been increasing, the elimination of iron-containing soils from our sanitary food supply, and our greatly reduced use of iron cooking vessels, have both contributed to the reduction in our iron intake.)

But there are at least three additional reasons for emphasizing iron nutrition: (1) the nutritional requirements for iron have increased in recent years as growth and maturation rates have accelerated; (2) the concentration of iron in the diet can provide a useful index of the overall quality of the diet; and (3) of particular relevance to the athlete, adequacy of iron has a direct impact on endurance and physical performance.

In short, there is less iron in our diet at a time when our needs are intensifying. What is more, we are not efficient in absorbing the iron that we do ingest.

IRON METABOLISM

Iron is metabolized in a unique way. The body has no normal mechanism for the excretion of significant amounts (with the exception of blood losses during menstruation). Instead, there is a mechanism which regulates the amount of dietary iron absorbed. The non-growing adult male has little need for iron and absorbs only about 10 per cent of the iron he ingests. Menstruating females have greater needs and absorb approximately twice as much. The ratio of absorption can be even greater in adolescent boys.

Approximately 85 per cent of the small amount of iron absorbed daily is used in the production of new hemoglobin, the pigment in red blood cells which gives them their color and transports oxygen. The remaining iron is used for growth of new tissues or is held in storage as a compound called "ferritin."

Growth demands of children are great, and in general they do not build up ferritin stores. In the average adult female, ferritin stores are about one-third as large as the male's, because of the iron demands of pregnancy and menstrual bleeding.

IRON NEEDS

A slight amount of iron is lost regularly from the exfoliated cells of the gut and skin, through losses of hair, and in minor quantities passed with bile into the small bowel. These combined losses generally run somewhat less than 1 mg. per day, so the average male adult need for iron (using a 10 per cent rate of absorption) is approximately 10 mg. per day.

Since iron losses in the female are greater, anywhere from 5 to 45 mg. during a menstrual period, daily requirements may be nearly twice as great—the RDA is 18 mg. per day. This is often more than the adult female will get in her average daily diet, and medicinal iron supplementation is frequently needed.

Growth imposes extraordinary demands for iron. During the adolescent years the normally larger needs of the female system are matched by the extraordinary needs of adolescent boys for their lean mass growth. During adolescence over 85 per cent of male growth is in lean body tissues, compared to 60 per cent for the average girl. As a result, the RDA for adolescent boys is approximately 18 mg. per day, about the same as the adult female.

Adolescent girls are more apt to be iron-deficient than boys. As indicated, their iron needs are comparable, but their over-all dietary needs are less. The growing boy, requiring and usually eating a large diet, will ordinarily get enough iron. Girls, on the other hand, who are generally more concerned with their silhouettes and exercise less, tend to eat less.

IRON IN THE DIET

Iron is found throughout a range of animal and plant tissues, and is widely distributed in the earth's crust. Animals often meet their own iron needs by ingesting substantial amounts directly from the soil (as when pigs and wild animals "root," or domesticated animals drink from muddy pools of water). Since the sanitary American diet has had the soil washed out, we are dependent upon the iron in the plant and animal tissues themselves.

For reasons not yet clear, humans absorb the iron in animal tissues (meat, fish, and poultry) more readily than the iron from vegetable sources. Furthermore, twice as much vegetable iron will be absorbed if it is eaten at the same meal with meat. Consequently, anyone on a vegetarian diet has to be particularly careful about getting enough iron. And supplementation with milk and milk products is not especially helpful, since they are poor sources of iron.

The table, Sources of Iron, shows the iron content of a list of common foods, organized in decreasing order of concentration.

In recent years the food industry has initiated the practice of adding iron to certain staples, notably wheat flour. These additional amounts are nutritionally significant, particularly in view of contemporary emphasis on baked products. Hopefully this practice will be upgraded, and even more iron will be added to these economically-priced staples.

INDIVIDUALS IN PARTICULAR RISK OF IRON DEFICIENCY

A common way of detecting anemia is through analysis of the concentration of hemoglobin in a small blood sample.

SOURCES OF IRON

FOOD	MEASURING UNIT	IRON (mg.)
*Liver—Pork	3 oz.	17.7
*Liver—Lamb	3 oz.	12.6
*Liver—Chicken	3 oz.	8.4
*Oysters, fried	3 oz.	6.9
*Liver—Beef	3 oz.	6.6
Dried Apricots	½ cup (12 halves)	5.5
*Turkey, roasted	3 oz.	5.1
Prune Juice	½ cup	4.9
Dried Dates	½ cup (9 dates)	4.8
*Pork Chop, cooked	3 oz.	4.5
*Beef	3 oz.	4.2
Dried Prunes	½ cup (10 prunes)	3.9
Tostada, bean	1	3.2
Kidney beans, cooked	½ cup	3.0
Baked beans with pork & molasses	½ cup	3.0
*Hamburger	3 oz.	3.0
Soybeans, cooked	½ cup	2.7
*Beef Enchilada	1	2.6
Raisins	½ cup	2.5
Lima Beans, canned or fresh cooked	½ cup	2.5
Refried beans	½ cup	2.3
Dried Figs	½ cup (4 figs)	2.2
Spinach, cooked	½ cup	2.0
*Taco—Beef	1	2.0
Mustard greens, cooked	½ cup	1.8
Corn tortilla, lime treated	8" diameter	1.6
Peas, fresh cooked	½ cup	1.4
Enchilada, cheese and sour cream	1	1.4
Egg	1, large	1.2
Sardines, canned in oil	1 oz. (2 medium)	1.0

*Foods of animal origin. Iron in foods of animal origin (except milk, which has little iron) is absorbed twice as efficiently as iron in foods of plant origin.

When dietary sources of iron are inadequate and iron stores exhausted, hemoglobin production is affected. (Recently developed methods of biochemical analysis provide a more critical assessment of iron status, identifying iron deficiency before anemia develops.)

A great deal of research has been undertaken to study iron deficiency. The results indicate that inadequate iron intake results in: loss of strength and endurance, easy fatigueability, shortening of attention span, loss of visual perception, and compromised learning ability. These findings make it imperative that the athlete found to be iron-deficient be treated specifically: he needs precise counselling and iron medication.

The data gathered in Washington as part of the Ten-state Survey included assessment of iron status of subjects grouped according to income levels:

THE WASHINGTON STATE NUTRITION SURVEY (1970)*

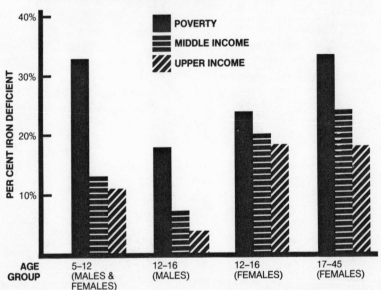

*Iron deficiencies determined biochemically, by measuring red blood cell porphyrin.

As the table demonstrates, over 30 per cent of the children 5 to 12 years of age from low-income families are iron-deficient. In contrast, active, rapidly growing boys 12 to 16 years of age and from high-income families almost always meet their needs for iron. Again, however, a high number, 20 per cent, of those living in poverty were found to be iron-deficient. Clearly the income level makes a significant difference. Iron-rich foods, particularly meats, are more expensive, and many low-income families simply cannot afford them.

Special concern should therefore be given to male athletes from low-income backgrounds. Their nutritional status should be evaluated in an effective testing program, and when found to be iron-deficient, they should be referred to a physician for definitive treatment.

Approximately 20 per cent of teen-age girls in the study showed biochemical evidence of iron deficiency. But there was basically no difference in the percentages among income levels. Girls from upper income families are iron-deficient to the same degree as girls from poor families. Low-income women between the ages of 17 and 45 reflected a higher deficiency percentage, but a substantial number, 20 per cent, of high-income women also showed evidence of iron deficiency.

Iron deficiency is rarely a problem among adult men. Their daily requirement is relatively small and is usually satisfied by their typically large intake of animal foods. If iron deficiency does occur, it usually means some form of blood loss. And the first medical concern should be for a bleeding lesion in the gastrointestinal tract.

THE PREVENTION OF IRON DEFICIENCY

Iron deficiencies in females are usually the result of either (or a combination of) their efforts to avoid high-caloric foods, simply not eating enough, or extraordinary menstrual losses. In the preparticipation health evaluation of girl athletes after the onset of menstruation, it is important to determine the presence or absence of iron deficiency. In addition to blood studies, a menstrual history should be taken. Those using intrauterine contraceptive devices which increase menstrual blood loss are at particular risk of a deficiency.

As previously mentioned, boys from low-income families should have their nutritional status evaluated as part of their pre-season physical examination. The first questions to ask a low-income athlete whose performance is less than expected are: "Is he getting enough to eat? Are his dietary needs for iron (and other nutrients) being met?" If not, an iron-rich diet should be prescribed. Iron-fortified cereal products, peas, beans, dark green leafy vegetables, and organ meats are good, inexpensive sources of iron.

A quality American diet will contain approximately 6 mg. of iron for every 1000 Calories. A diet well selected from the Four Food Groups, if adequate in calories, can contain sufficient iron to meet the needs of growing boys and most girls.

SUMMARY

An adequate intake of iron merits particular concern. Iron status can be tested, deficiencies are common, it can affect the entire well-being of the person concerned, and most particularly, athletic performance.

Although vegetable foods contain iron, absorption is less efficient than it is for animal foods; however, the efficiency of absorption of vegetable iron is increased if vegetables are eaten together with meat, fish, or other animal products.

As a rule females are more apt to be iron-deficient than males. Teen-age boys from poverty families are also at particular risk. Deficiency among adult males is rare, and when it occurs, it very probably reflects blood loss.

The RDA for adolescents is 18 mg. of iron per day. The need remains relatively constant for females until they stop menstruating, whereas the need for adult males drops to approximately 10 mg. per day when growth stops.

It is a good general rule to test all athletes at the beginning of training for possible iron deficiencies. Women and teen-age boys from low-income backgrounds warrant special concern.

The iron-deficient athlete, once identified, needs a thorough medical evaluation and treatment under a physician's supervision.

SUGGESTED READINGS AND REFERENCE WORKS

1. Smith, N.J. and Rios, E.: "Iron Metabolism and Iron Deficiency." *Adv. in Pediatrics,* 21:239, 1975.

2. Monsen, E.R., Kuhn, I.N. and Finch, C.A.: "Iron Status of Menstruating Women." *Am. J. Clin. Nutrit.,* 20:842, 1967.

eight

THE PRE-GAME MEAL AND EATING DURING COMPETITION

Athletes have lots of excuses for losing. They may feel unprepared, badly coached, short-changed by the officiating, or handicapped by some injury or illness. But they seldom have a clear explanation for why they win. They usually end up with generalities, like, "I had a good day . . . ," or, "things sure felt good today. . . ."

Out of this inability to articulate reasons for winning has grown a mythology about pre-competition eating, which has little basis in fact. Many runners regard pizza as a "fast" food, while soccer players the world over demand bacon and eggs before a game. In this country, numerous athletes, particularly football players, feel unprepared for competition without a game-day ceremonial steak dinner, with baked potatoes, dry toast, and tea.

IMPORTANT FACTORS IN PRE-GAME EATING

There are endless bizarre stories of pre-game eating practices. Most of them not only reflect confusion, they add to it. Take the well-known account of a young lady swimmer who broke the world's record for the 200 meter butterfly after a pre-race meal of two hamburgers with onions, french fries and ketchup, a root beer, three brownies, and a candy bar. It is usually told as a nutrition horror story. Actually the meal wasn't all that bad, and it was considerably better than some of the eating practices which have become traditional in American sports. Her meal was low in fat and high in carbohydrate; it was eaten well before the race, and it was food she enjoyed and was familiar with. She could have done worse.

There was the much worse example of three varsity swimmers who went to their apartment during the noon break of a conference swimming meet, and ate steaks, potato chips, French bread, and ice cream. In the early afternoon events, one swimmer won and set a new conference record, one swam his worst time of the season, and the third never finished. What accounted for their varying reactions? Obviously, different individuals react differently to any one dietary regimen (complicating any effort to formulate specific rules). Nevertheless, it is possible to set general guidelines which should be helpful to all athletes. Some indiscreet practices can be disastrous, and a good pre-game diet program can help avoid them.

One factor that will always be present, and a primary consideration, is the nervous tension. The more important the competition, and in many cases the more successful and intense the competitor, the greater is the tension leading up to and surrounding the actual event. Women are no less affected than men, often much more. Appetites are often finicky and stomachs unsettled. What are the physiologic bases for such pre-game reactions?

At times of stress and tension there is a striking decrease in blood flow to the stomach and small intestine, along with decreased motility of the stomach and small bowel. These changes contribute to the general lessening of interest in food and liquids. Induced by nervous tension, there may also be increased motility in the lower intestinal tract, with resulting diarrhea.

Individual likes and dislikes are apt to become more accentuated. People who generally eat almost anything suddenly develop pronounced feelings about what foods they can and cannot tolerate. The fact that these are purely psychological factors makes them no less real, and any pre-game diet must take such personal preferences into account.

THE GOALS OF THE PRE-GAME DIET

The following goals should be considered in planning the pre-game diet:

1. Energy intake should be adequate to ward off any feelings of hunger or weakness during the entire period of the competition. Although pre-contest food intakes make only a minor contribution to the immediate energy expenditure, they are essential for the support of an adequate level of blood sugar, and for avoiding the sensations of hunger and weakness.

2. The diet plan should ensure that the stomach and upper bowel are empty at the time of competition.

3. Food and fluid intakes prior to and during prolonged competition should guarantee an optimal state of hydration.

4. The pre-competition diet should offer foods that will minimize upset in the gastrointestinal tract.

5. The diet should include food that the athlete is familiar with, and is convinced will "make him win."

The traditional steak breakfast or midday banquet fails to meet many of these goals. Its high protein content will compromise hydration; the high fat content will delay the emptying of the stomach and upper intestinal tract; and the low-carbohydrate content will fail to support the glycogen and glucose stores necessary for immediate energy and a good level of blood sugar.

All too often the steak "brunch" has represented the only game-day meal. One varsity football player said recently that the best thing about making the first team was that it kept him busy on the field. Sitting on the bench, he had had the chance to think about how hungry he was; and by the fourth quarter he was usually so famished that he got headaches.

Except for this one day in the week large and active young football and basketball players are used to a regular schedule of eating every two to four hours. Their bodies are not about to agree that there is something special about game day that makes food unnecessary for seven or eight hours.

FOOD INTAKE BEFORE COMPETITION

For most competitors the best diet plan provides modest amounts of high-carbohydrate foods, taken at regular intervals up to within two and a half hours of the competition. As stated earlier, the carbohydrates will provide the quickest and most efficient source of energy, and have neither the slow gastric emptying problem of fats nor the dehydrating tendency of protein.

In addition, the trainer or coach planning pre-game meals should insist on the following: (a) that athletes do not miss meals, (b) that food intake is regular, and (c) that massive intakes shortly before competition are avoided. Other than these general rules, a considerable amount of individual leeway is possible and desirable.

Some competitors will prefer soup and light sandwich meals, others cold cereal eaten with sugar, skimmed milk, and perhaps fruit. Large meals with fatty meats are usually a poor idea. And again, it is essential that athletes not skip meals, particularly the early meal on the day of competition. The fewer the deviations from regular eating schedules, the better.

Again, it should be emphasized that individual food preferences are all-important in the intense periods prior to competition. Athletes will continue to believe that particular foods help make winners, and even if they violate some of the principles laid down above, there should be every effort to provide as much latitude as possible. The psychological factors are of overriding importance. When the athlete believes that pizzas, persimmons, or paté de fois gras will make him win, his digestive system will probably cooperate, and he will be mentally prepared for a top performance.

FLUID INTAKE BEFORE COMPETITION

The third goal of pre-game eating is maintaining an optimum state of hydration. To achieve this, fluids are important—not only before and during the contest, but for two or three days beforehand. The immediate pre-game diet should include two to three glasses of some beverage (and today's youth must sometimes be reminded that "beverage" includes water). Whole milk is not recommended, because of its high fat content (and many cannot tolerate large milk intakes). Caffeine-containing beverages, such as coffee and tea, may present problems for the very young athlete, who is unaccustomed to the effects of caffeine. Caffeine stimulation can increase the nervous tension and agitation prior to a contest, and is often followed by feelings of depression. Non-carbonated, fruit-flavored drinks are generally good. They are liked by most athletes, and they provide some sugar; and they are particularly helpful during those competitions which go on for a prolonged period of time.

The Liquid Pre-Game Meal

Originally developed for hospital patients, there are highly nutritious and very palatable liquid formulas on the market which can work very well for pre-game meals. Such commercial products as Ensure®, Sustagen®, and SustaCal® can satisfy all of the requirements for pre-competition foods. They are high in carbohydrate, come in readily accepted flavors, and can contribute to both energy intake and hydration. They also contain sufficient fat and protein to give a feeling of satiety and relieve hunger, but because they leave the stomach promptly, they can be taken in small amounts up to within a few minutes of competition.

For many athletes the idea of getting their needed nutrients in liquid meals may seem strange. Therefore, they should not be served for the first time on the day of the big game. There should be first a period of instruction and experimentation during the training season. Liquid meals should be used before competition only when the athletes understand their nutritional advantages, and only if they have come to accept them.

The large football breakfast has been around for a long time. It should be displaced with care. If given a chance, competitors will respond to new ideas and good information; and they will be willing to learn that the bloody meat of the pre-game steak is not necessary for virility and endurance. The University of Nebraska football team was effectively weaned to liquid pre-game meals, and flourished on the field.

As might be expected, there have been instances where overenthusiasm for the liquid pre-game meals has led to unfortunate complications. If extra protein or carbohydrate is added to the products described above, the higher concentrations can cause cramping and diarrhea. Similar complications have arisen in attempts to use commercially available breakfast substitutes, or reducing formulas which are high in protein and low in calories. As a general proposition, the preparation of liquid meals should be left to the professional nutritionists and food technologists.

There has also been a tendency at times to extend the use of the liquid meals to everyday diets. This is not a good idea. These foods are expensive, and their regular use detracts from eating programs which will help to increase awareness of sound nutritional principles.

MEETING THE NEEDS OF ENERGY AND HYDRATION DURING COMPETITION

Hydration and energy are the main considerations during competition, particularly in those events that extend over a period of several hours. Track and swimming meets, tennis tournaments, and wrestling competitions all demand that the athlete compete several times during one extended period, and measures insuring good hydration become particularly important.

As stated previously, the pre-game meal should contain two to three glasses of fluids, and hourly intakes of fluid should be scheduled during competition. The athlete's preference for fruit juices or noncarbonated soft drinks should be followed, and, once again, there is also water.

Regularly scheduled fluids can meet the needs for the maintenance of energy. In the competitions extending over several hours there is a need for additional sources of energy to maintain high blood sugar levels and carbohydrate stores in the liver. Fruit juices, chilled and diluted with equal volumes of cool water, can meet these needs very well. Drinks containing glucose (described in Chapter 5 in connection with the High Performance Diet) are very good sources of energy, as long as the glucose concentration is not too high. Some athletes prefer these drinks in the frozen form of ices or popsicles to suck on intermittently throughout the day.

FEEDING THE TRAVELING TEAM

The principles of satisfying nutritional requirements are no different on the road, but it is often more difficult to carry out the program effectively. The key is advanced planning. The five goals of the pre-game diet outlined above can be met in commercial establishments, if arrangements are made in advance with hotel and restaurant managers. It is often important to order special menus, and to make arrangements for feeding at precise (and often irregular) times. The well-informed trainer or manager will be aware that the average restaurant fare is high in fat, protein, and salt, and will find ways to make the necessary arrangements.

The major pitfall for the traveling team is overeating. There is usually a reduction in normal training activity and a surplus of free time, when eating and snacking become popular ways of relieving boredom. Athletes should be made aware of this problem and urged to limit their food intake.

Weight-control sports may pose additional problems. Here, of course, there will be need for special care in the advance arrangements and planning of the meals. The traveling wrestling team provides the classic example, because, in addition to the problems faced by any travelling team, weight control is essential. The following is a sample menu for food available in most commercial restaurants and hotels, which permits wrestlers to maintain weight while providing sufficient energy stores:

Breakfast

8 oz. orange juice
1–3 Eggs
Toast or French toast
8 oz. skimmed milk
(Ham, sausage, and bacon should be
    avoided because of their high salt content.)

Lunch

Sandwiches (one or two)
    Turkey, chicken, beef, or hamburger
    (Avoid corned beef, ham,
        luncheon meats, and salami.)
Sherbet, ice cream, jello, or fruit
Coffee, tea (if appropriate), 8 oz. skimmed
    milk, fruit juice, or a carbonated beverage.

Dinner

6–8 oz. meat (no ham)
Potato or rice
Vegetable
Jello salad
Dinner roll
Sherbet, ice cream, or fruit
Coffee, tea (if appropriate), 8 oz. skimmed
    milk, fruit juice, or a carbonated beverage

This menu is probably adequate for most traveling teams, although it can be supplemented with high-glucose drinks or liquid meals for those who have a higher energy demand, particularly at snack time in the evening. It is better to err on the side of not providing quite enough food away from home. A light snack can always be added for the athlete who really gets hungry, but it is next to impossible to get a stuffed overfed athlete or team "up" for high-level competition.

It is worthwhile mentioning again the special hydration problems posed by jet flight. If the flight lasts more than an hour or two, there should be special provisions for fluids: two or three glasses an hour immediately before, during, and after a flight. In case of long transcontinental travel, an extra day or two at the destination before competition will help establish good levels of hydration.

LOW-COST PRE-EVENT MEALS

Most teams, particularly high school teams, do not have to worry about jet travel and hotel eating. Budgets usually call for car pools and school buses, and food is taken from home or the school cafeteria. The pre-event meal needs can be met very adequately, at times superlatively, with the foods planned and prepared at home or at school. Sandwiches, fruit juices, fruits, and hard candies can be provided in a "brown bag" meal.

Of course, simple principles of good nutrition must be kept in mind. It is important to avoid mayonnaise and spreads which may be high in fat and susceptible to spoilage without refrigeration. It is advisable to stay away from high-salt snack foods, such as chips and salted nuts, and to have an abundant supply of noncarbonated drinks available prior to competition. Once again, the "brown bag" meal should cater to individual food preferences. The trip itself is no time to experiment with new and strange concoctions, regardless of their theoretical merit.

SUMMARY

There is considerable confusion about which foods are best for pre-game meals and competition. Many unusual diets have been associated with high-level performance, and unfortunately cherished habits change slowly. The traditional pre-game steak meal continues, but is gradually being recognized as less than desirable nutritional preparation for competition.

The pre-game meal should provide sufficient energy to minimize hunger and weakness; ensure a proper state of hydration; insure prompt emptying of the upper gastrointestinal tract; avoid inducing gastrointestinal upset; and, above all, reflect the athlete's preferences.

In general, frequent small intakes, often in liquid form, can best meet these needs. Carbohydrate foods should be emphasized. They not only contribute to energy needs, they also leave the stomach promptly and are readily absorbed. Several commercial liquid meals have proved useful in pre-event feeding.

The traveling team presents particular problems, most of which can be solved with adequate pre-planning and advance arrangements. A major problem of the traveling team is over-eating, particularly on extended trips. Hydration can be of particular concern in jet travel. The problems of local travel can be easily met, if proper care and planning are involved in the preparation of the food and liquids needed for the trip and the competition itself.

SUGGESTED READINGS AND REFERENCE WORKS

1. Hirata, I.: "Pre-Game Meals," *The Jour. of Sch. Health,* p. 409, Oct., 1970.

2. Benarde, M.A.: *Bacterial Food Poisoning in Our Precarious Habitat.* Chapter 3. W.W. Norton & Co., New York, 1973.

nine

WRESTLING AND OTHER WEIGHT CONTROL SPORTS

"You can always spot the members of our wrestling team by the middle of the season. Their clothes don't fit and they fall asleep in class."

The above was heard recently from a high school chemistry teacher. With no minced words, he neatly summarized exactly what's wrong with the majority of wrestling programs in high schools and colleges all over the country. During the competitive season, wrestlers often have severe nutritional problems.

One of them recently visited the Sports Medicine Nutrition Clinic. The nutritionist who saw him emerged from the consulting room with a perplexed look: "That young man I've just been talking to can't be a University student; he couldn't deliver an intelligible sentence." The appointments clerk knowingly replied, "He's a straight-A student, but he's on the wrestling team. And it's Friday. He hasn't had anything to eat or drink for two days."

THE EFFECTS OF
INADEQUATE WEIGHT PROGRAMS

What are the results of such abuse? Sports medicine and physiology literature report innumerable studies of weight control programs and their effect on strength and endurance. In general, they have reported that "making weight"—losing up to 5 per cent of body weight in two or three days—does not adversely affect performance. But such conclusions have been reached under the limited conditions of the tests. What the real effects may be in actual competition is another matter.

Who knows what the outcome might have been for the wrestlers who faded badly in the third period, particularly when they were required to wrestle repeatedly during a one- or two-day meet? The wrestlers themselves know the effects of starvation and dehydration on scholastic and general social effectiveness.

It is an article of faith that wrestlers perform most effectively at their lowest possible weight. But do they? There is some experimental evidence to the contrary. And there is nutritional common sense which says that you cannot seriously dehydrate the body and deprive it of food, and expect it to perform most effectively. The weight that is lost during the typical crash period at the end of the week, when the team members can no longer study because they feel "thick-headed," is water loss. And that can mean severe dehydration.

National sports organizations are aware of this situation. At least one medical society has passed a resolution recommending that wrestling be dropped at the high school level. This would be a real and unnecessary loss. Wrestling is an exciting and demanding sport, serious injuries are rare, it rewards good conditioning, and allows a boy of any size to compete. It is now among the fastest growing sports in high school and college, involving over 300,000 competitors each year. But, as suggested above, it has raised problems. In particular, the unenlightened attitudes toward weight and weight control require review.

One of the outstanding members of a university team provides a typical example of the weekly weight ordeal. Wrestling at 128 pounds, he has competed regularly for six years. He was a state champion in high school and is now a strong contender for national honors at the college level. As a first step in helping him establish a sound weight-control program. he was asked to keep careful records of his food intake for one week during the season. It looked like this:

COLLEGE WRESTLER—
WEIGHT AND FOOD INTAKE, BEFORE COUNSELING

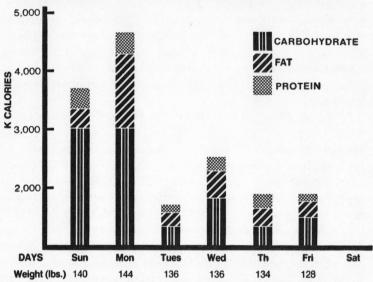

After making weight and wrestling at 128 pounds on Saturday, this wrestler and his equally dehydrated and hungry teammates headed for a nearby drive-in. There they consumed large quantities of soft drinks and drive-in-quality barbecued sandwiches with potato chips. On Sunday, he ate one meal in the middle of the day which included chicken, a vegetable, a salad, and dessert. During the remainder of the day, he studied, ate 38 Ritz crackers, drank 40 ounces of lemonade, and snacked on rolls, jam, and apples. His caloric intake for the day was 2685 Calories.

On Monday he ate three meals: a breakfast of milk and cereal, a lunch of a soft drink and tamales, and a steak dinner. With candy snacks throughout the day, his caloric total came to 3661 Calories. By Tuesday he weighed 144 pounds and was suddenly confronted by the fact that he had to lose 16 pounds by Saturday.

So he reduced his food intake sharply. On Tuesday his diet contained only 630 Calories—from one meat pie, a cherry cola, and an apple. His weight was 136 pounds on Wednesday morning. He avoided breakfast and lunch, but on Wednesday evening he met a friend and had a ham dinner, containing 1580 Calories. His weight stayed at 136 pounds on Thursday. He ate a small fish dinner on Thursday and took in no fluids. By Friday his weight was down to 134 pounds. On Friday he had one can of soft drink and 20 shortbread cookies, which contributed a total of 826 Calories. By Friday afternoon he was still six pounds overweight.

As was his custom, he spent Friday afternoon in the sauna, remaining there until he could no longer sweat. Then he put on two sweat suits and a rubber suit and ran until he had lost five of the last six pounds. He lost the last pound in the traditional manner: by spitting into a mason jar. He went home and refrained from eating or drinking anything until the weigh-in on Saturday morning.

This wrestler's regimen was frightening enough. But at least it did not involve laxatives or diuretic "water pills," the use of which has become all too common. Nonetheless, he went into his match badly depleted of water and the carbohydrate stores necessary for the desired level of energy, strength, and endurance. He won this particular match, but as had happened quite consistently in the past, he was outpointed in the last period.

The wild fluctuations in this wrestler's weight were due mainly to changes in his body water. He was expending approximately 3000 Calories a day, and even if he had eaten no food between Tuesday and Saturday, he would have lost less than three or four pounds of body fat over the four-day period. Since he actually took in about 4000 Calories in that period, even on his restricted diet, his net loss of body fat could have been no more than three pounds. The remaining 13 pounds, which was lost between Tuesday and Saturday, was entirely made up of body water. Because this story is typical, high school and college wrestling is earning the dubious title of "the internal water sport."

An important factor was the salt in the young man's diet. The barbecued roast beef sandwiches and chips on Saturday, the Ritz crackers on Sunday, and the mid-week ham dinner were all high in salt content, accentuating water retention and weight gain. (The emphasis on salt in his eating was not surprising, after the induced sweating and salt loss at the end of the preceding week.)

There is a better way to control weight. The first step is to determine the ideal competing weight for each wrestler. (Methods of calculation are discussed later in this chapter.) Once the competing weight is reached, a diet program for weight maintenance can be readily devised. It should ensure an adequate intake of nutrients, allow for optimum levels of hydration, and offer a caloric intake appropriate to meet the competitor's high needs.

THE HIGH PERFORMANCE DIET

The wrestler described above required about 3000 Calories a day. His needs were met through a combination of the Basic Diet (Chapter 2) and, for important competition, the High Performance Diet. (The High Performance Diet, as described in Chapter 5, is particularly well suited for wrestling, because it provides the glycogen stores and carbohydrate intake necessary to meet the very strenuous energy demands of a wrestling match.) He was told to eat as much as he wanted to satisfy his appetite early in the week, as long as he restricted his carbohydrate intake to approximately 110 grams per day. Towards the end of the week the restriction on carbohydrate foods was removed, and the diet was supplemented with a high-carbohydrate glucose drink. To help him make weight, he was instructed to avoid the high salt-containing foods listed in the box, and bulky foods with high residue; it is helpful if food residues in the bowel are minimal for weigh-in and competition.

The "Weight and Food Intake Chart After Counseling" reflects the dramatic changes in his diet and weight fluctuations: The wrestler was able to satisfy his appetite, meet his energy needs, and stabilize his weight for competition. He

HIGH SALT-CONTAINING FOODS

The following foods should be limited in the diet for 72 hours prior to competition or weigh-in in weight control sports. Very modest intakes are permissible, but large servings will result in water retention. Water intakes should be generous during this period: no less than eight full glasses each 24 hours:

Anchovies
Bacon and bacon fat
Bologna
Bouillon cubes
Bread and rolls with
  salt topping
Catsup
Celery salt, onion
  salt, garlic salt
Cheese (all kinds)
Chili sauce
Chipped and corned beef
Cottage cheese (salted)
Crackers
Dry cereals
Frankfurters
Ham
Herring
Horseradish
Kosher meat

Luncheon meat
Meat tenderizer
Mustard
Olives
Peanut butter
Potato chips, corn chips
Pretzels
Relish, pickles
Salt, Monosodium glutamate
Salt pork
Salted nuts and popcorn
Salty and smoked fish
Salty and smoked meats
Sardines
Sauerkraut
Sausage
Soups (canned)
Soy sauce
Worcestershire sauce

had a highly successful year, both in wrestling competition and academically. And he particularly impressed the coaching staff by becoming a strong third-period performer.

Most competitors will not want to follow the High Performance Diet all the time. It should be limited to periods immediately preceding the most important competitions, particularly the tournaments and critical events toward the end of the season.

A repeated reminder: by participating in crash weight-loss programs, wrestlers are not significantly altering the fat

COLLEGE WRESTLER—
WEIGHT AND FOOD INTAKE, AFTER COUNSELING

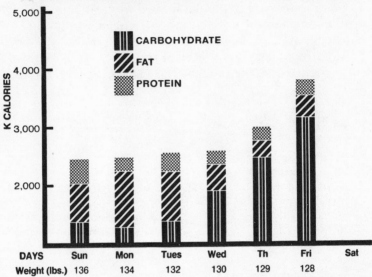

DAYS	Sun	Mon	Tues	Wed	Th	Fri	Sat
Weight (lbs.)	136	134	132	130	129	128	

and tissue content of their bodies; they are simply altering the water and salt content. Most competitors expend at least 3000 to 4000 Calories each day during the training and competition seasons. This caloric intake permits a generous diet, which will satisfy hunger, provide strength and endurance, and cause no unwanted weight gain.

THE IDEAL COMPETING WEIGHT

How does one determine a given individual's ideal competing weight? We have discussed the popular belief that a competitor will wrestle most effectively at his lowest possible weight; the emaciated participants found on many wrestling teams (seldom the champions) bear witness to this fallacy. Research has shown that the most effective weight for competition is one where there is a healthy and effective level of hydration, optimal muscle mass, and no excessive body fat.

What is the recommended level of body fat? Several recent studies approached this question by evaluating the body composition of wrestling champions. Their average body fat was approximately 5 to 7 per cent. Efforts are underway to develop a relatively simple system for determining appropriate weights based on these fat percentages. (This makes much more sense than trying to define optimal weights on the basis of height and weight relationships.)

The simplest method of estimating body fat is through measurement of skin fat fold thickness. This simply requires a pair of skin-fold calipers and a conversion table with which to estimate the percentage of total body weight represented by fat tissue. These measurements can be effectively utilized to establish the minimum (and most effective) weight for each wrestling team member. A wrestler may wish to compete in a heavier weight class, but if he attempts to wrestle below a minimum based on his skin fat fold estimate, he will most likely compromise his wrestling ability—and possibly his health.

A typical 16-year-old American high school boy who weighs 156 pounds can be expected to have a body fat composition of 15 to 17 per cent of his total body weight. The 10 per cent he would have to lose in order to reach an optimum level of 5 per cent would be approximately 15 pounds (10 per cent of his 156 pounds). If this estimate is made at the beginning of the school year, a necessary allowance should also be made for an increase in muscle mass from the regular wrestling conditioning program. In all, he should lose approximately 15 pounds of body fat and gain three to five pounds in muscle mass, a net loss of 10 to 12 pounds. His optimal wrestling weight would be 145 pounds.

As is true of all weight reduction programs, the critical factors are, first, sufficient time, and secondly, increased energy expenditure—along with reduced caloric intake. No program should require a loss in excess of four pounds per week; two pounds is generally more desirable. Since each pound of fat lost requires a caloric deficit of 3500 Calories, the active athlete who can raise his daily caloric expenditure up to 3500 Calories can follow a Basic Diet of 2000 Calories and lose two to three pounds per week. *An intake of 2000 Calories each day should be the minimum allowed for an athlete involved in a vigorous training program.* This will provide the necessary nutrients and minimal energy needed for academic performance, daily activities, growth, and training.

THE ESSENTIALS OF A WEIGHT CONTROL PROGRAM

The essentials of an effective weight control program for wrestling may be summarized as follows:

1. The estimation of optimum weights and weight-loss needs for all competitors should be made shortly after school begins in the fall. The basic method is the skin fat fold measurement, and the recommended level of body fatness for competition is 5 to 7 per cent. This early determination of proper weight for competition will provide a period of up to ten weeks for weight reduction, which should be ample. (By the simple device of plotting out on a piece of graph paper the present weight and the desired weight, and connecting the two by a line, the appropriate rate of weight loss can be easily projected. A sample form for this procedure can be found in Appendix C.)

2. Instructional materials should be made available to all the athletes, advising them on the essentials of diet, foods, energy balance, caloric density, need for increased exercise, etc. The highly motivated scholastic wrestler is keenly interested in learning the facts which will enable him to participate more effectively. (There is an example of instructional material for the wrestler in the Appendix.)

3. Parents should be advised about the program, particularly if it calls for weight reduction on the part of

their son. It is important that they understand the dangers of "cutting weight," as well as the dangers of excess fatness; they should have a clear understanding of how they can cooperate to insure that the weight reduction program will enhance the health of the participant.

4. Athletic directors, school administrators, and other concerned members of the school staff must be kept informed of the program. Surprisingly, there is a common misconception that it is unhealthy for young boys to be involved in weight reduction. To the contrary, any weight level that is appropriate for a wrestling program must be one consistent with optimal health, and thus will serve to improve the fitness and overall health of the young people involved.

5. Special attention must be paid to members of the football team who expect to participate in wrestling. They will generally be among the heavier members of the team, and will often end the football season with a higher than desirable percentage of body fat and a relatively brief period of time for weight loss. Since their dietary intakes should not be less than 2000 Calories, they will often need special training programs (often 2-a-day workouts) to insure sufficient weight loss. But in any event, these programs should not call for a rate of loss in excess of four pounds per week. Here again, it is important that these individuals know the nutritional implications of weight control; they are particularly vulnerable to the temptations of ill-advised crash diet programs.

6. Holidays present particular problems for weight control programs. It is traditional to eat more, to eat more foods with high caloric density, and to avoid the regular schedule of workouts over the holidays. (In many states weight certification takes place in early December, and a sudden weight gain over the Thanksgiving recess can seriously jeopardize weight

qualifications for the season.) In many states, if a high school wrestler competes at a higher than certified level in one match, he must continue to compete at that weight during the remainder of the season. Therefore, it may be important to continue scheduled workouts and have weigh-ins during the holiday season. If weight loss is required immediately after the holidays, there may be a need for a special program of vigorous exercise and dietary restriction (limited caloric intake, and avoidance of bulky and high-salt foods).

It is worth repeating that weight control programs do more than improve athletic performance. In contrast to the starvation diets and unnatural weight fluctuations of most wrestling programs, the weight levels advocated in this chapter contribute to all-around general health. By American middle-class standards, these levels may appear to be on the light side. But in terms of optimum health they are not. Well-conditioned high school wrestlers with 5-7 per cent of body fat should be the most fit students in the school.

GROWTH DEMANDS OF THE
HIGH SCHOOL WRESTLER

The high school years are, of course, a time of vigorous growth, and any weight control program must allow for the needs of that growth.

Cutting weight through crash dieting and erratic eating arrests growth during the wrestling season. After the season the participants generally appear to "catch up" in growth, without evidence of permanent stunting. But it is clear that general health was compromised during this period, and whether permanent physical damage can be documented seems beside the point. Whatever else happens, athletic performance is bound to suffer.

Growth rates for high school boys vary greatly, and average about ten pounds per year—or approximately three pounds during the third of the year represented by the wrestling season. In most states regulations allow for a weight gain of one to two pounds during each of the winter months, and this should adequately allow for normal growth. Greater increases will usually represent an unwanted addition of fat tissue.

Although there is great variation among individuals, the average college competitor has usually achieved his adult growth. With proper control of caloric intake, he can expect to maintain a stable weight throughout the season. The Basic Diet will provide optimally for his needs, as it does for the high school wrestler's. And the High Performance Diet will help him prepare for special competition.

OTHER WEIGHT CONTROL SPORTS

The principles applicable to weight control for wrestlers are valid for participants in all sports where weight control is important. The healthy level of 5 to 7 per cent of body fat can be recommended to any young competitor who wishes to achieve the best possible weight for competition. (Although the data is much more limited with regard to weight control sports for women, the information available to date suggests that a level of 5 to 7 per cent is also commonly found among female champions in many active sports—despite the fact that women generally have a higher level of body fat than men.)

Light-weight crew is another popular college sport which has specific weight restrictions. The light-weight oarsmen can weigh no more than 159 pounds, and the total crew average cannot exceed 155 pounds. Unlike wrestling, there is no range of weight options; and often an oarsman who cannot make the heavy-weight crew will be tempted to try out for light-weights. If he weighs 175 pounds and has a trim 5 per cent fat level, he should be advised not to attempt the necessary

16-pound weight reduction. However, if his estimated fatness is 12–15 per cent, he can be counseled through a healthy weight reduction program to achieve qualifying weight.

Anyone experienced with light-weight crew programs will eventually begin to wonder whether they are designed to broaden the base of competition or whether they are really a test of the ability of highly motivated large individuals to see how small they can get and still propel a boat a given distance through water.

Again, in addition to the problems of those trying to lose too much, there are those who try to lose too fast. Take the individual who is carrying 10 to 15 per cent body fat and tries, in a very brief period of time, to reduce to the qualifying weight for light-weight crew. During training very active crew members will often expend as many as 5000 Calories per day. Under these circumstances, a maximum healthy rate of weight loss can be reached on a 2500-Calorie diet. And this may have to be adjusted upward if, as is frequently the case, the training program calls for a daily expenditure of at least 6000 Calories.

Again, a weight loss of four pounds per week should be the maximum. This requires a daily deficit of about 2500 Calories, and if 5000–6000 Calories are being expended, 3500 should be ingested. And to repeat once more, weight-loss programs must begin early enough. Candidates for the light-weight crew should be identified during the winter, or at least many weeks before weigh-in, so they will have plenty of time to reach desired weights by the beginning of rowing season.

The coxswains present some very interesting and special problems. Since they do not have the rowers' needs for strength and endurance, their prime consideration is maintaining a body weight as close to the minimum as possible (111 pounds). If they become overzealous in reaching and maintaining the exact minimum weight, they can jeopardize both their own general health and the effectiveness of the crew. As leader of the boat, the coxswain can play a very significant (and sometimes negative) role. Too often an irritable half-starved coxswain, who hasn't had anything to eat or drink for 24 to

36 hours, can have a devastating effect on the competitive spirit of the whole boat.

It also appears that coxswains are particularly vulnerable to overdoses of vitamins and nutritional supplements. Like so many athletes, they often tend to take such unnecessary supplements, and because of their small size, they are particularly susceptible to the risk of toxic overdoses.

DIURETICS AND CATHARTICS

Both wrestlers and light-weight crew members are often tempted to resort to the use of diuretics and cathartics—the former to increase urinary water losses, the latter to remove food residue and water from the intestinal tract.

Both diuretics and cathartics cause water loss and consequent dehydration, which can directly inhibit the production of energy. In addition, they both remove significant amounts of potassium from the body. Potassium is necessary for muscle function; and the "washed out" feeling of weakness following an attack of diarrhea is due in large part to the loss of potassium and body water.

The adverse effects of the cathartics are usually obvious, and one experience is frequently enough. The results of the diuretics are not so apparent, and the urinary losses of water and potassium can actually result in life-threatening shock. These agents have no place in weight programs, and their abuse can result in serious muscle weakness and total collapse.

SUMMARY

Achieving optimal weight for a weight control sport can have a very positive effect on the overall health and well-being of the competitor. The average middle and upper-middle class high school participant frequently has an excess of body fat, and a reduction in fatness to the 5 to 7 per cent range will enhance both general health and athletic performance.

On the other hand, sudden and severe losses of body weight are unhealthy and counterproductive. They usually represent only massive shifts in body water, which can only compromise performance.

A carefully designed program, which reduces body fat to an estimated 5 to 7 per cent of total body weight, often requires a significant period of time. And the loss should usually be limited to between three and four pounds a week. It should be accompanied by an adequate exercise program, so that nutrient intakes can be sufficient to meet body needs. A 2000-Calorie weight reduction diet should be minimal.

Allowances should be made for normal growth processes; and high school wrestlers should be expected to gain two to four pounds in lean body mass during the season. Gains in excess of these amounts may represent increase in body fat.

The common apprehensions and misinformation of administrators and parents can frequently be dealt with through a program of consultation and education before weight reduction programs are implemented.

Cathartics and diuretics to increase weight loss are never justified. Not only do they hurt athletic performances, they can critically endanger health.

SUGGESTED READINGS AND REFERENCE WORKS

1. Tipton, C.M. and Tcheng, T.K.: "Iowa Wrestling Study: Weight Loss in High School Students." *J.A.M.A.,* 214:1269, 1970.
2. Katch, F.I. and Michael, E.D.: "Body Composition of High School Wrestlers." *Med. Sci. in Sports,* 3:190, 1971.

ten

NUTRITION FOR THE ELEMENTARY SCHOOL ATHLETE

There weren't always organized sports for all ages. Only in recent years have we seen this development, and there are now programs and leagues for participants ranging the gamut from the very young to the very old. This chapter will consider the youngest athletes, whose training, conditioning, and competition are all too often as intense as those of the high school or college competitor.

With the age-group expansion of organized sports, it is now common practice for 8- to 10-year-olds to be members of teams which require active participation three or four times a week. This obviously requires dedication, but the over-zealousness on the part of many parents carries it to abusive lengths.

At the end of a recent lecture to a group of health workers and parents, the floor was opened to the typical question-and-answer period. After some delay, a woman raised her hand and asked, "Is vomiting harmful to children?" She was urged to elaborate. With obvious concern, she did just that: "My son plays in an organized football program, and when he can't make his weight limit, my husband puts his finger down his throat several times to make him vomit." That opened the floodgates of questions: "Do water pills hurt 12-year-olds making weight for football?" "What about children sweating off weight in rubber suits?" "Are hormones dangerous?"

All of these practices can be physically harmful, to say nothing of the psychological factors that are obviously involved. Nonetheless, such shocking abuses are disturbingly widespread. And they have prompted great concern over the desirability of highly competitive team sports for the very young. There is no doubt that many programs for elementary-age children have been carried too far, particularly those community-based activities directed by nonprofessional volunteers. While the school activities are usually organized and administered with trained professional guidance, the community programs are frequently run by frustrated former athletes and would-be coaches. With limited knowledge and seemingly less concern for the well-being of the participants, their unquestioning thesis appears to be that being made to win is good for everyone.

These excesses are often ruining programs that could be both enjoyable and educational. Not only can they teach skills, they can also contribute to better health; and they provide excellent opportunities for teaching young people the basic principles of nutrition.[1]

THE BEGINNINGS OF GOOD HEALTH HABITS

Unfortunately, the main home-based activity of many young American children is watching television; and it's a sad start toward lifelong sedentary habits. The lack of exercise at this age can be as harmful as it is later. The inactive overweight child stands too good a chance of becoming the fat adult.

This problem is due in large part to the lack of opportunities for attractive exercise. A well-devised athletic program can change a vicious cycle into a positive self-reinforcing one. More exercise brings a better appetite, an ability to eat more without adding fat, and a sense of accomplishment in learning athletic skills. A good program for the young child can develop beneficial habits for a lifetime. With proper guidance the

[1]In response to the concern about the athletic programs for this age group, the subject has been reviewed by the American Academy of Pediatrics, the American Medical Association, and the Society of State Directors of Health, Physical Education and Recreation. A statement has been issued and a copy may be obtained from the American Association for Physical Education and Recreation, 1201 Sixteenth St., N.W., Washington, D.C. 20036.

relationship between selective eating, regular exercise, and health doesn't need to be taught; it's repetitively discovered through experience.

With this in mind, it is extremely important to develop programs which are enjoyable for a wide range of children. Too often school and community activities exalt male-oriented, highly competitive sports, which so rarely take into account the particular needs of girls approaching their prepubescent years. Just at the time when adolescent growth is making extraordinary nutritional demands, social pressures are often pulling in the wrong direction.

Rather than exercise, the average American girl is directed to relatively sedentary activities and/or told that a good figure requires (excessively) limited calories. The results are clearly unhealthy. Any elementary school athletic program can help reverse these trends by encouraging both boys and girls to exercise actively and to eat properly.

DIET RECOMMENDATIONS FOR THE ELEMENTARY SCHOOL ATHLETE

The principles of sound dietary practice can be taught to people of all ages. And the best overall advice to the elementary school athlete is simply to follow the Basic Diet and eat a good variety from the Four Food Groups, in amounts dictated by hunger. The necessity of pleasant surroundings for eating was pointed out earlier, and is particularly important in this age group. This usually means a pleasant family mealtime—not eating in front of TV.

There is considerable variation in the ages at which puberty starts—and with it, the period of rapid growth and high nutritional demands. Prior to puberty, nutritional needs are quite modest. And the belief of many parents that these younger children should eat more to "build up strength" is clearly fallacious. Indiscriminate eating won't build up their strength; and it may, in fact, be the start of a lifelong struggle with obesity.

Recent examples of extraordinary achievement by the very young have no doubt influenced many parents to hope for early athletic development in their children. In international swimming competitions particularly, top performance in the early teens has almost become the general rule—with the result that many lose their zest for competition and retire by the time they are 18. These, of course, are cases of unusual early development; and they can only provide distorted examples to parents of children who do not mature as early. Those parents must learn that the eventual maturity and prowess of their children doesn't necessarily depend upon how early they begin adolescence; that in any event, the process won't be affected by diet; and that efforts to force-feed can do no good (and indeed may reduce effectiveness on the playing field).

The emphasis on diet should be low-key, assuring regular mealtime eating, and teaching the basic importance of a varied food intake in providing the range of nutrients required for health and development. It is not the age to get into such practices as the High Performance Diet, nor the time for particular emphasis on special foods or food groups—to say nothing of extraordinary diet supplements.

The one specific influence the coach or parent can exert usefully is to discourage high-calorie snack foods. Depending upon the stage of the child's growth and his level of activity, such foods may or may not pose a real problem. But they certainly will some day, and this is an excellent time to start the education process.

The other area in which special attention may be necessary is in connection with hydration, particularly in hot weather. Principles discussed in Chapter 6 are equally applicable for the younger group.

NUTRITIONAL ABUSES OF THE YOUNG ATHLETE

As well-meaning as their intentions may be, a large number of coaches and parents have supported various practices which are threatening to both physical and emotional health. Some of these abuses, such as the emphasis on high-pressure regional and all-star competition, are not within the province of this book. Hopefully critics will be available to help focus attention on these and related abuses and to orient the community to the real recreational needs of this age child.

An enlightened parent can help identify the abuses of the overenthusiastic adults in his community, and help foster the well-informed and controlled enthusiasm any program will benefit from. It will suffice here to summarize common nutrition-related practices which have a direct bearing on the health and well-being of the young people involved:

1. Weight control is an important health problem, even in the elementary school child. But the concern for overweight youngsters can be carried too far. The enthusiastic parent or coach who attempts to "run some fat off" the chubbier team members can be harmful, even dangerous. Frequently the exercise demands are too sudden and too extreme, such as running laps in extra clothing during hot weather. Fatigue to the point of collapse and dangerous heat exhaustion can be the results. The obese youngster who wishes to participate in athletics should have a medically supervised weight control program, not a crash diet to make weight for the community football team.

2. Football and baseball programs are often scheduled for the hot, humid months of the year. When the humidity is over 90 per cent and the temperature is higher than 85°F., there should be no hesitancy in postponing a practice or game. When humidity and temperature approach these levels, there is a real danger of heat exhaustion. Particular care should be given to provision for light-weight clothing and the availability of ample fluids, during any form of physical exertion in hot weather.

3. Use of special dietary supplements and drugs, and the initiation of weight-lifting programs, have found their way into the elementary-age sports programs. Such hormone agents as "Dianabol" have been given to young people to improve muscle mass and, supposedly, athletic performance. For this age group in particular, they are highly dangerous, can permanently stunt normal growth, and may cause testicular damage. Sedatives and stimulants are also used. Again, it doesn't require detailed argument to point out the dangers involved in all of these practices. There is no place for these agents in any athletic program.

SUMMARY

In our sedentary society there is real need for sports programs at all levels, and good programs can be of great benefit to the pre-adolescent child. In addition to providing enjoyment and exercise, and teaching particular game skills, these programs can be used to motivate the initiation of sound nutritional practices.

Unfortunately there are many adults who teach a win-at-all-costs attitude. This approach builds up unnecessary pressures and often leads to a variety of specific abuses. Any parent or child involved in sports programs should be aware of such abuses and take proper steps to avoid them.

Young girls have special needs. They can benefit particularly from healthy energy-expending programs and should not be excluded from them. If they are introduced to athletics at an early age, it can help them develop the active lifestyles which will keep them in shape throughout life.

The nutritional requirements of the young athlete can be met by the Basic Diet. It should be remembered that excessive food doesn't build strength or endurance. Generous amounts, however, are healthy, and the calories are easily expended by the average child. If there is a real weight problem, a professionally supervised program should be followed.

As with adults, heat exhaustion is a common problem with children. This can and should be prevented. Drugs, dietary supplements, and special diets must be eliminated from grade school programs.

eleven

FITNESS FOR THE OLDER ATHLETE

A few minutes on any busy street corner will tell the story about American fitness after the age of 20. Most adults have probably been exposed to sound nutritional information at some point in their lives, but it has obviously gone unheeded. Two hundred thousand Americans die of heart attacks each year before their sixty-fifth birthday. Half the women in the country have compromised their health with obesity, and the men have an even more serious problem.

There are, of course, exceptions. Several mornings each week a group of 40- to 60-year-old men gathers at a neighborhood athletic field for a program of calisthenics and running. Trim, vigorous, and easily capable of strenuous exercise, they are indeed an impressive group. They are clearly enthusiastic about the program and enjoying themselves.

This is not an unusual story. Such groups are common throughout the country—suburban middle-aged men involved in programs of exercise and dietary restraint, which have rewarded them with vigor and youthful good looks extraordinary among their contemporaries. They are postcoronary attack victims participating in carefully designed rehabilitation programs. They are among the two-thirds of heart attack victims who have survived their first attack.

It's a telling commentary on the state of contemporary middle-aged fitness that these men should stand out. In the predominantly rural America of the past, considerable physical activity was needed just to maintain a home and make a living. Even the urban office worker at the turn of the century expended more physical energy walking to the streetcar, firing his furnace, tending his horse, walking to the store, and climbing his stairs than does the average "exercise buff" of today. More often than not the latter gets his exercise by driving his sports car to the local athletic club, where he rides an elevator to his workout.

Even the concept of spectator sports has changed drastically. Our grandparents might have spent a typical Sunday afternoon watching a ballgame—from the grandstands, after they had walked to the stadium. Today's spectator watches the game on a television screen, a few feet away from a well-stocked refrigerator, with a remote control device which saves him from getting out of his comfortable chair to adjust the set.

Even people who are involved in strenuous athletic programs don't seem to be getting the message so far as lifelong exercise and fitness are concerned. Nothing shows this quite so vividly as the homecoming reunion of the great old football team of 25 years ago. Most of us have seen them out on the football field for the half-time ceremonies: overweight and unfit, no one would be so indiscreet as to suggest that they try to run the length of the field. In their fifties, they must represent a goodly portion of their teammates who can only receive their applause "in memoriam."

In a recent report on American football players who made *Who's Who in American Sports,* only 65 per cent lived past the age of 50. The average age of death was 57.

THE DECLINE OF FITNESS

Through recent surveys we have been able to gather a considerable amount of data on American adults and where they stand with regard to physical fitness. Attention has focused more on men than on women, primarily because men have proved more susceptible to early degenerative diseases of the heart and blood vessels, making them far more prone to heart attacks and strokes. If one assumes that the average young man leaves college in a state of relative good health and fitness (an assumption not warranted for far too many), it is possible to trace typical patterns of degeneration in the ten years or so immediately following.

Often first priority goes to establishing a career. The pressures of the new job seem to preclude the establishment of a regular exercise program. Long and irregular hours, travel, and the expense-account lunch are hardly conducive to thoughts of a workout after work.

Until quite recently military obligation was a regular part of postschool life for most young men. Contrary to the image in the recruiting posters, and probably in the minds of most of the folks back home, it tended to be a fitness disaster. Once past basic training, military life for the majority involved too much food and too little exercise.

The other common experience of young men is marriage and the start of a family. This too has not been conducive to regular exercise. The living pattern of the average young family tends to revolve around indoor recreation, with emphasis upon culinary triumphs, and little disposition to spend those free moments out on the jogging path or tennis court.

As income increases with age, costlier (often fat-laden) foods become more prominent in the diet. Alcoholic consumption and smoking tend to increase, often in association with the growing tensions of making one's mark in the commercial world. Erratic schedules lead to a dependence upon on-the-run snacks and the gradual disappearance of the sit-down family meal.

A DIET FOR ADULT FITNESS

The diet for the over-25 athlete must meet the basic requirements of a diet at any age. That is, it must supply all essential nutrients, but not caloric intakes in excess of expenditure. Beyond these general rules are some that apply to more specific groups; i.e., a limitation on animal fat in the adult diet, and progressively reduced caloric intake with advancing age.

Heart attacks and coronary vascular catastrophes are striking greater numbers of American adults every day. More prevalent among males than females, these dangers are too clear for any of us to ignore. The following are guidelines for a prudent diet advocated by the American Heart Association:

1. Follow a diet that meets the daily needs for protein, vitamins, minerals, and other essential nutrients. This can be readily done, without providing excessive calories, by selecting foods appropriately from the Four Food Groups. From the dairy group, emphasize skim milk and skim-milk cheeses, as well as other foods low in fats.

2. Select foods that will be eaten. A diet considered a penance will be short-lived. This does not mean that eating habits can't be improved, but it does mean that within the rich abundance and variety of foods available to most Americans, nutritional needs can usually be met without sacrificing any of the enjoyment of eating.

3. Control calories and maintain desirable weight. This, again, is the critical factor in food intake. Keep in mind that a useful guide for many people is the weight they carried between the ages of 20 and 25, assuming they were in reasonably good shape. This general rule does not work for all, however. A former linebacker who played at 228 pounds now weighs 172 and is healthy and in excellent shape. In contrast, a former halfback from the same team is still at his playing weight of 175 pounds. As an overcommitted business executive, he gets little exercise; and he doesn't realize that his original fatness level of 12 to 15 per cent has now risen to over 35 per cent.

    After 50 or 60, almost all people benefit from a reduction from the caloric intakes of those earlier years.

4. Be aware of the two danger areas of sugar and fats. The danger of sugar lies primarily in its "empty"

calories. Sugar-rich food can certainly be eaten by the healthy adult, but in moderation. Fats are associated with many of the common diseases of middle-aged Americans, most notably heart disease. American consumption of fat now represents roughly 45 per cent of total caloric intake. This compares with approximately 25 to 30 per cent a generation ago, at a time when the more active lifestyle of the average American made him better able to accommodate substantial fat in his diet. The moral is to stay away from fatty foods in selecting the discretionary portion of the diet, after the standard servings from the Four Food Groups.

5. Of the fat that is eaten, choose polyunsaturated rather than saturated fats. As discussed in an earlier chapter, polyunsaturated fats are generally liquids of vegetable or fish origin. Fats that are solid at room temperature, such as those associated with red meats, butter, etc., are saturated and should be avoided.

The following menu plans incorporate these suggestions:

1400 CALORIE DIET   **1800 CALORIES**

Breakfast

½   cup prune juice   + 1 T. honey
⅔   cup oatmeal
½   cup skim milk
1   corn muffin
1½ teasp. margarine
     tea or coffee (with skim or
        low-fat milk)

Total Calories: 425

Lunch

6   oz. tomato juice   + ½ cup plain yogurt
     cold chicken (½ breast)
     celery sticks
1   slice whole wheat bread

1½ teasp. margarine
½ cup fresh fruit salad, *or*
1 piece fresh fruit

Total Calories: 390

Dinner

Baked white fish (3 oz.)
  with rice herb stuffing
  (½ cup)
½ cup green beans
6 oz. baked squash
½ cup orange sherbet
  tea or coffee (with skim
  or low-fat milk)

Total Calories: 570

+ 1 cup cream of mushroom
  soup
+ green salad with 1 T. Fr.
  dressing
+ 1 cookie

Total additional Calories: 390

Total Daily Calories: 1385   **Total Daily Calories: 1775**

To increase the 1800-Calorie diet to 2000, add 1 carton fruit yogurt (250 Calories) as a snack or allow two more servings of bread with a small amount of margarine.

Cholesterol and Saturated Fat in the Diet

The last recommendation (of the Heart Assoc.) is extremely important, since there is considerable evidence associating cholesterol and saturated fats with coronary vascular disease. The following guidelines can be helpful in reducing the intake of cholesterol:

1. Eat no more than three egg yolks per week, including the eggs used in cooking.

2. Limit the use of shrimp and organ meats; they are high in cholesterol.

3. Emphasize fish, chicken, turkey, and veal in the meat meals, restricting beef, lamb, pork, and ham to no more than two or three times per week.

4. Eat only lean cuts of meat, trimming off the solid

visible fat; and discard the fat that cooks out of the
meat.

5. Avoid deep-fat frying. Instead use cooking methods
that help remove fat, such as baking, boiling, broiling,
roasting, and stewing.

6. Restrict the use of fatty luncheon and variety meats,
such as sausages, salami and sandwich meats.

7. Instead of butter and other cooking fats that are solid
or completely hydrogenated, use liquid vegetable oils
and margarines that are rich in polyunsaturated fats.

8. Instead of whole milk and cheeses made from whole
milk and cream, use skim milk and skim-milk cheeses.

ALCOHOL IN THE ADULT'S DIET

In the United States the per capita consumption of alcohol
is increasing every year. Alcohol has no place in the diet of
an athlete during competition; and in the adult diet it represents, in addition to its social problems, a substantial and
often unrecognized source of calories.

Alcohol itself contains 7 Calories per gram, nearly as
much as fat. It is often consumed with snacks of high caloric
density, such as nuts and dips. Furthermore, alcohol may lead
to increased eating. If alcoholic consumption is a regular part
of life, even in moderation, there will be that many more
calories in the daily diet to offset, increasing the need for
a regular exercise program.

DECREASING ENERGY NEEDS
OF THE OLDER ADULT

The metabolic rate of all adults gradually decreases after their
mid-twenties, thereby reducing their caloric needs. The
amount and rate of such reduction will vary from person to
person, and each individual must monitor himself to find the
eating level that will maintain proper weight. A useful guide

for many is to reduce the caloric intake by 100 to 150 Calories per day for each decade after the age of 25.

The failure to recognize this decreasing energy need is a substantial cause of the obesity prevalent among older people. An excess of only 100 Calories a day will contribute a pound of fat per month, 24 pounds in two years. Two hundred Calories per day, a martini and a handful of nuts, will create the problem in a year.

PHYSICAL ACTIVITY

Assuming good health, the range of exercises for adults is almost unlimited. If his or her program is consistent and well planned, the middle-aged executive can actively participate in the marathon run, the martial arts, or strenuous hikes. Too often, of course, exercise programs are undertaken in moments of sudden resolution, notoriously in the first hours of each new year. Men who have limited their exercise to pushing elevator buttons suddenly acquire rubber suits and decide to "run off some pounds." This is asking for trouble. Although in most instances the result will simply be disillusionment, a serious threat to the musculo-skeletal and cardiac systems is sometimes very real.

If a person has not been exercising regularly, he or she should start by talking to a professional who is trained in helping devise appropriate exercise programs for adults. Good professionals can be found in physical education departments of most schools, through the family physician, or at the local Y.M.C.A. or athletic club. If necessary, one can also write to the President's Council on Physical Fitness in Washington, D.C.

It is absolutely essential that exercise programs be carefully planned to accommodate the physical limits of the participants, that they involve a regular schedule, and, most important, that they be enjoyable. There are too many demands on the average person's time to allow for an exercise program of much value if it isn't enjoyed; it will be followed sporadically if at all, and that's not enough. For even the most conscientious individual, trying to meet energy-expending exercise needs by not taking elevators or "doing the yard work" is rarely adequate. There is simply not an exercise base in the daily routine to build on, so the exercise program itself must call for enjoyable, planned activity.

THE DIET FOR THE
SERIOUS ADULT COMPETITOR

Serious competition for seniors is becoming widespread. Age-group swimming, track, and tennis competitions are rapidly growing in popularity; and the older athlete will often have questions as to how to prepare nutritionally for such demanding events.

First of all, the adult athlete who is competing regularly must be in sound physical condition. He should get sufficient regular exercise to permit a more ample diet than would be appropriate for his more sedentary counterpart. He should participate in consistent workouts and not try to get by on the natural athletic ability with which he dazzled the world many years ago.

The adult diet outlined above should be adequate for his needs. Under extremely competitive circumstances, the High Performance Diet (see Chapter 5 and the Appendix) can be effective—but probably not for the participant over 40. The glycogen-loading of cardiac muscle has been thought by some to be dangerous for the older individual.

Day-long events require good hydration and continuing carbohydrate supplies, just as they do for the younger competitor. Regular intake of fluids, high-carbohydrate snacks (like sweetened juices and hard candies), and light lunches of foods such as chicken sandwiches and sherbet will usually provide what is needed.

However, the adult athlete may experience a problem not shared by the younger participant: an intolerance to sugar. The enzymes located in the lining of the intestinal tract, which are needed for digestion of sucrose, lose their effectiveness with age. The undigested sugars remaining in the intestinal tract cause abdominal discomfort, distension, and intestinal gas. Great individual variation will be experienced in this regard, and the adult athlete will learn how to take his carbohydrate in small doses, with adequate fluids to maintain good hydration.

SUMMARY

The average American adult is not in condition for serious competition, or even a vigorous exercise program. The demands of daily living are inconsistent with regular exercise, and eating habits have become nutritionally inadequate.

A prudent diet for the adult American is essentially a variation on the Basic Diet. There should be an adequate intake of all essential nutrients, with a decrease in saturated fats, cholesterol, and sugar. Alcohol consumption should be moderate.

Since age brings a progressive slowing of the metabolic rate, less and less calories are needed with advancing age. Generally speaking, there should be a 100- to 150-Calorie reduction per day for each ten-year period after the age of 25.

A program of planned, regular, and enjoyable exercise is necessary. For the older adult who has not exercised regularly, professional guidance is strongly recommended.

For the serious senior competitor, the dietary needs are little different than for the younger athlete. Carbohydrates may be less easily tolerated; and the High Performance Diet is generally unadvisable for athletes over 40.

A program of prudent dietary intake and regular exercise will pay significant dividends in both athletic performance and good health.

twelve

A WORD ABOUT SOME SPECIFIC SPORTS

We've emphasized that food intake influences body size and composition and also provides energy; and as different sports call for different physical attributes and different energy resources, food needs can be specific for individual sports. This chapter will summarize some of these specific needs, particularly with reference to the problems commonly encountered in counseling athletes in some of the more popular sports. References to the text will aid in the location of the pertinent discussions there.

BASKETBALL

Basketball is generally played by the tall (and the very tall), who rarely have problems of over-fatness, at least not until after their competitive days are over. Frequently the tall, thin basketball player will wish to gain weight, particularly for effectiveness in the contact aspects of the game. As pointed out in Chapter 4, this can only be accomplished over significant periods of time, ideally with a programmed schedule calling for a gain of one to two pounds weekly. It should be undertaken during the off season, when supervised weight-training and specific muscle-building exercises will not interfere with the development of the skills of the game.

The pre-game meal for the basketball team presents certain unique challenges. The six- to seven-foot active athlete needs a great deal of energy, i.e., food. Basketball games are often played in the evening. The tradition of a final large meal at 2 o'clock in the afternoon may have satisfied the needs of smaller, less active basketball players a generation ago; but it will send today's basketball player into the game hungry, short on energy resources, and often with deficient hydration. The principles outlined in Chapter 8 will assure a good level of hydration, and can definitely help improve performance. The liquid pre-game meal in particular is well suited for basketball competition.

SWIMMING

Many competitive swimmers train intensely throughout most of the year. Many are young and still growing. Thus, understanding and eating a sound Basic Diet (Chapter 2) is most important. Both training and competitive performance can be optimized by a good diet, and the swimmer who eats properly will be less susceptible to "going stale."

A light carbohydrate intake before the routine early-morning workout is often well tolerated; i.e., juice and one or two muffins with jam or honey. The swimmer, especially when involved in two-a-day workouts, will probably not do well on the snacks and one-meal-a-day eating schedule so common among high school and college students. Three meals (with additional snacks if desired), dividing energy intake somewhat evenly throughout the day, is usually better. Preparation for competition for events of varying duration involves the principles discussed in Chapter 5; in particular, the "High Performance Diet" has proved beneficial to competitors in the middle distance and longer races.

CREW

Participation in crew presents the challenge of training for many months during the year (September thru June) but competing intensely in relatively few races (during the spring months). The Basic Diet (Chapter 2) is important for optimal performance during training. In addition, there should be some fluid and carbohydrate intake within a couple hours of heavy workouts—either in the early morning or early afternoon.

Rowing in competition is the most intense energy-expending sport per unit of time. Thus the High Performance Diet (Chapter 5) can be particularly helpful.

As a weight-controlled sport, lightweight crew poses particular weight control problems, and nutritionally sound solutions are critical for effective competition. The applicable principles are outlined in Chapter 9.

The high energy demands of rowing make it particularly important that women crew members take care to avoid iron deficiencies. All girls seriously competing in rowing should have a pre-participation laboratory evaluation of their iron status. The problem of iron nutrition, as discussed in Chapter 7, is therefore of particular importance to oarswomen, and there is a separate discussion of their requirements in Appendix F.

TENNIS

In recent years, tennis players have come into the Clinic to be counseled about a host of common nutrition problems, including most particularly weight control, high-energy meatless diets, and the need for nutrient supplements. Problems somewhat unique to the tennis player result from the fact that competition often involves long tournaments, when two or three matches may be played on one or more consecutive days, many times during hot weather. Players are concerned about their energy resources over these extended periods, and the maintenance of good hydration can (and always should) be a prime concern. Regularly scheduled fluid intakes, sufficient to maintain constant weight from same day to day during several days of a tournament, are critical. Eating regular meals, as close to a normal schedule as possible, and supplementing with sweetened drinks or candies throughout the day of competition, should insure proper electrolyte balance and necessary energy (Chapters 6, 8).

GYMNASTICS AND FIGURE SKATING

Although both men and women participate in these sports, diet-related problems are far more common among the women. Again, iron nutrition needs must be met (Chapter 7), but weight control is the major concern. Over-fatness is a real handicap for both the gymnast and the figure skater. Many aspects of the intense training for these sports do not require large expenditures of energy, and on even modest caloric intakes, some of these girls cannot lose—or may actually gain weight. There are of course always some whose intake isn't so modest. Weight reduction programs compatible with good athletic performance (Chapter 4) can be helpful; it is particularly important to assure that an increase in caloric expenditure (i.e., exercise) is part of the program.

FOOTBALL

Three nutrition-related problems dominate any consideration of football: first, the life-threatening problems of hydration and heat induced disease, particularly in warm weather (Chapters 6, 10); secondly, gaining weight to improve performance (Chapter 4); and finally, the regulation of food and fluid intakes on game day, i.e., the pre-game meal (Chapter 8). The maintenance of a healthy level of body fatness in later adult life is a particular problem for the former football athlete (Chapter 11).

TRACK AND FIELD, CROSS COUNTRY

The participants in the track and field events encounter the entire range of energy demands—from the purely ATP-PC energy-expending effort in the high jump to the predominantly aerobic demands of the long-distance races (Chapter 5). Optimum preparation for different events will differ. The distance runners, including those running cross country, can benefit from the alternately low and high carbohydrate intakes of the High Performance Diet (Chapter 5), and all should be familiar with the American College of Sports Medicine statement on "Prevention of Heat Injuries During Distance Running" (Appendix E).

Weight control problems are usually limited to the shot putters and discus throwers, who seek to gain body mass—and thus increased strength. (They may or may not be enhancing their performance with such efforts; more study is needed documenting the true relationship between increased body mass, strength, and performance in these events.) At any rate, we do know that any weight-gaining program should be supervised under diet and exercise conditions outlined in Chapter 4. Anabolic steroids (Dianabol®) and Periactin® are used with disturbing frequency by the weight throwers. Their use is dangerous and unethical.

WRESTLING

Chapter 9 is devoted entirely to the important nutrition-related implications of this popular sport. If the widespread starvation, fluid deprivation, and induced dehydration are not brought under effective control soon, this fine sport may well be eliminated, at least at the high school and junior high school level.

HIKING, MOUNTAINEERING, CROSS-COUNTRY SKIING

Increasing numbers of our citizens of all ages are "taking to the hills" for sport and recreation. Their efforts will be rewarded through increased enjoyment and added health and vigor, if they understand and apply the fundamental principles of the energy-producing mechanisms (Chapter 5). The more intense the effort, the more essential the assurance of adequate supplies of water and concentrated sources of carbohydrates. Scheduled fluid and food intakes are essential to the pleasure and the success of a challenging climb (Chapter 6). Basic principles of good mountaineering require a check of the purity of water sources at lower altitudes, and a generous estimate of fuel requirements for melting snow for drinking water at high altitudes.

These popular sports are representative of most of the activity patterns (and thus the nutrition-related needs) of practically all sports. For example, the needs of the soccer and the ice hockey player for prolonged anaerobic energy sources are quite similar to those of the basketball player; their needs for pre-game foods and regular fluid intakes are also similar (Chapters, 6,8). The needs of ice skaters are similar to those of swimmers and runners. Bicycle road-racers must have both anaerobically and aerobically derived energy in their long races—their energy needs are similar to those of distance runners.

FOOD AND NUTRITION BOARD, NATIONAL ACADEMY OF SCIENCES–NATIONAL RESEARCH COUNCIL
RECOMMENDED DAILY DIETARY ALLOWANCES,[a] Revised 1974

Designed for the maintenance of good nutrition of practically all healthy people in the U.S.A.

	Age	Weight		Height		Energy	Protein	Fat-Soluble Vitamins				Water-Soluble Vitamins			
								Vita-min A Activity		Vita-min D	Vita-min E Activity[e]	Ascor-bic Acid	Fola-cin[f]	Nia-cin[g]	Ribo-flavin
	(years)	(kg)	(lbs)	(cm)	(in)	(kcal)[b]	(g)	(RE)[c]	(IU)	(IU)	(IU)	(mg)	(μg)	(mg)	(mg)
Infants	0.0–0.5	6	14	60	24	kg×117	kg×2.2	420[d]	1,400	400	4	35	50	5	0.4
	0.5–1.0	9	20	71	28	kg×108	kg×2.0	400	2,000	400	5	35	50	8	0.6
Children	1–3	13	28	86	34	1,300	23	400	2,000	400	7	40	100	9	0.8
	4–6	20	44	110	44	1,800	30	500	2,500	400	9	40	200	12	1.1
	7–10	30	66	135	54	2,400	36	700	3,300	400	10	40	300	16	1.2
Males	11–14	44	97	158	63	2,800	44	1,000	5,000	400	12	45	400	18	1.5
	15–18	61	134	172	69	3,000	54	1,000	5,000	400	15	45	400	20	1.8
	19–22	67	147	172	69	3,000	54	1,000	5,000	400	15	45	400	20	1.8
	23–50	70	154	172	69	2,700	56	1,000	5,000		15	45	400	18	1.6
	51+	70	154	172	69	2,400	56	1,000	5,000		15	45	400	16	1.5
Females	11–14	44	97	155	62	2,400	44	800	4,000	400	12	45	400	16	1.3
	15–18	54	119	162	65	2,100	48	800	4,000	400	12	45	400	14	1.4
	19–22	58	128	162	65	2,100	46	800	4,000	400	12	45	400	14	1.4
	23–50	58	128	162	65	2,000	46	800	4,000		12	45	400	13	1.2
	51+	58	128	162	65	1,800	46	800	4,000		12	45	400	12	1.1
Pregnant						+300	+30	1,000	5,000	400	15	60	800	+2	+0.3
Lactating						+500	+20	1,200	6,000	400	15	80	600	+4	+0.5

[a] The allowances are intended to provide for individual variations among most normal persons as they live in the United States under usual environmental stresses. Diets should be based on a variety of common foods in order to provide other nutrients for which human requirements have been less well defined. See text for more detailed discussion of allowances and of nutrients not tabulated. See Table I (p. 6) for weights and heights by individual year of age.

[b] Kilojoules (kJ) = 4.2 × kcal.

[c] Retinol equivalents.

	Water-Soluble Vitamins			Minerals					
	Thiamin (mg)	Vitamin B$_6$ (mg)	Vitamin B$_{12}$ (µg)	Calcium (mg)	Phosphorus (mg)	Iodine (µg)	Iron (mg)	Magnesium (mg)	Zinc (mg)
Infants	0.3	0.3	0.3	360	240	35	10	60	3
	0.5	0.4	0.3	540	400	45	15	70	5
Children	0.7	0.6	1.0	800	800	60	15	150	10
	0.9	0.9	1.5	800	800	80	10	200	10
	1.2	1.2	2.0	800	800	110	10	250	10
Males	1.4	1.6	3.0	1,200	1,200	130	18	350	15
	1.5	2.0	3.0	1,200	1,200	150	18	400	15
	1.5	2.0	3.0	800	800	140	10	350	15
	1.4	2.0	3.0	800	800	130	10	350	15
	1.2	2.0	3.0	800	800	110	10	350	15
Females	1.2	1.6	3.0	1,200	1,200	115	18	300	15
	1.1	2.0	3.0	1,200	1,200	115	18	300	15
	1.1	2.0	3.0	800	800	100	18	300	15
	1.0	2.0	3.0	800	800	100	18	300	15
	1.0	2.0	3.0	800	800	80	10	300	15
Pregnant	+0.3	2.5	4.0	1,200	1,200	125	18+ [h]	450	20
Lactating	+0.3	2.5	4.0	1,200	1,200	150	18	450	25

[d] Assumed to be all as retinol in milk during the first six months of life. All subsequent intakes are assumed to be half as retinol and half as β-carotene when calculated from international units. As retinol equivalents, three fourths are as retinol and one fourth as β-carotene.

[e] Total vitamin E activity, estimated to be 80 percent as α-tocopherol and 20 percent other tocopherols. See text for variation in allowances.

[f] The folacin allowances refer to dietary sources as determined by *Lactobacillus casei* assay. Pure forms of folacin may be effective in doses less than one fourth of the recommended dietary allowance.

[g] Although allowances are expressed as niacin, it is recognized that on the average 1 mg of niacin is derived from each 60 mg of dietary tryptophan.

[h] This increased requirement cannot be met by ordinary diets; therefore, the use of supplemental iron is recommended.

appendix b

ALTERNATE BASIC DIET SAMPLE MENUS

5 MEALS

Breakfast

½ cup citrus segments
1 shredded wheat biscuit
1 cup skim milk

Snack

1 hard-boiled egg
2-3 wheat crackers

Lunch

1 cup vegetable soup
1 slice cheese bread
1½ teasp. margarine
1 apple or other fresh fruit

Snack

1 carton fruit yogurt

Dinner

3 oz. broiled hamburger
1 broiled tomato parmesan
    green salad with French
    dressing
⅔ cup risotto with peas
1 cup skim milk or
    other beverage

Total calories: about 1500

3 MEALS

Breakfast

½ cup grapefruit juice
1 scrambled egg
1 slice whole wheat toast
1½ teasp. margarine
1 cup skim or low-fat milk
    or other beverage

Lunch

1 cup chili con carne
    carrot sticks
1 serving fresh fruit
1 cup skim or low-fat milk

Dinner

3 oz. (no bone) veal cutlet
    with pan juices
⅔ cup mashed potato
½ cup zucchini
½ cup apple crisp
1 cup skim milk or other
    beverage

Total calories: about 1450

172

WRESTLER'S WEIGHT-LOSS GRAPH

This is the weight reduction graph provided for a 16 year old high school junior preparing for the wrestling team. He weighed 155 pounds and had an estimated level of fat of 15% of his body weight. It was recommended that he compete at 145 pounds, on the basis of a 10% reduction of body fat (15 pounds), and assuming he would increase his muscle mass by 5 pounds through training.

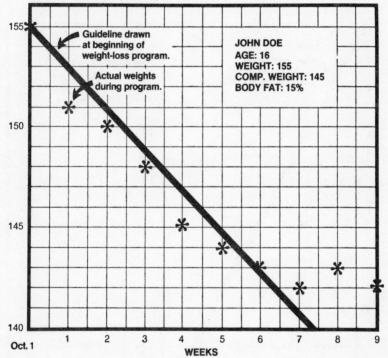

Guideline drawn at beginning of weight-loss program.

Actual weights during program.

JOHN DOE
AGE: 16
WEIGHT: 155
COMP. WEIGHT: 145
BODY FAT: 15%

WEEKS

Oct. 1

FOOTBALL PLAYER'S WEIGHT-LOSS GRAPH FOR WRESTLING

This high school senior, weighing 178 pounds, was a member of the football team and had an estimated level of fatness of 18%. It was recommended that he wrestle at 165 pounds. On a strict 2000 Calorie diet, with morning running and afternoon workouts, he reduced his body fat to 6% and his weight to 162 pounds by the first weigh-in five weeks after the end of football season.

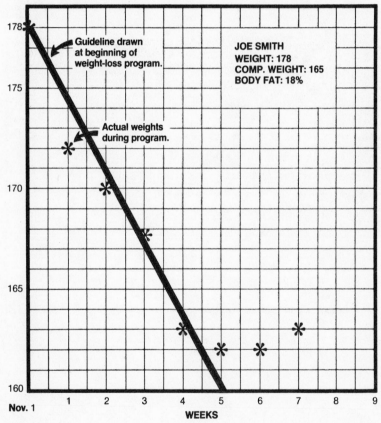

Guideline drawn at beginning of weight-loss program.

Actual weights during program.

JOE SMITH
WEIGHT: 178
COMP. WEIGHT: 165
BODY FAT: 18%

WEEKS

appendix d

MEASUREMENT WITH A SKINFOLD CALIPER

The degree of body fatness can be measured simply and accurately by measuring skinfolds at appropriate sites, and using calipers specially designed for the purpose. (The photograph shows a measurement being made with the Lange Skinfold Caliper, manufactured by the Cambridge Scientific Industries, Cambridge, Maryland.)

With appropriate conversion tables, obtainable from the supplier, the per cent of body fat can be ascertained quickly and easily.

The following are triceps skin-fat-fold Obesity Standards for Caucasian Americans (adapted from Seltzer, C. C. and Mayer, J., "Simple Criteria of Obesity," *Postgraduate Medicine,* 38:101–107, 1965):

SKIN-FAT FOLD (IN MILLIMETERS)

AGE (YEARS)	MALE	FEMALE
5	12	14
7	13	16
9	15	18
11	17	21
13	18	23
15	16	24
17	14	26
19	15	27
21	17	28
23	18	28
25	20	29
27	21	29
29	23	29
30-50	23	30

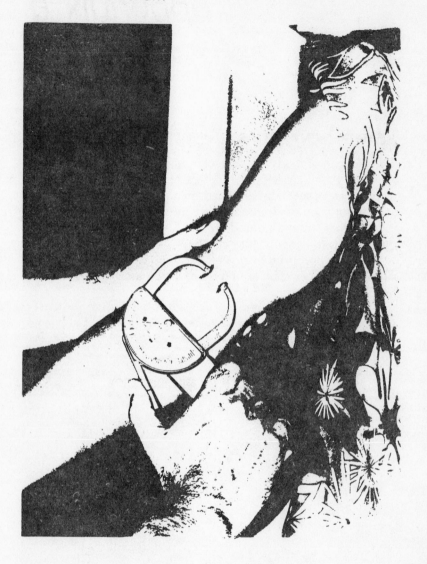

appendix e

ACSM POSITION STATEMENT ON PREVENTION OF HEAT INJURIES DURING DISTANCE RUNNING

Based on research findings and current rules governing distance running competition, it is the position of the American College of Sports Medicine that:

1. Distance races (> 16 km or 10 miles) should **not** be conducted when the wet bulb temperature—globe temperature* exceeds 28° C (82.4° F). (1,2)

2. During periods of the year, when the daylight dry bulb temperature often exceeds 27° C (80° F), distance races should be conducted before 9:00 A.M. or after 4:00 P.M. (2,7,8,9)

3. It is the responsibility of the race sponsors to provide fluids which contain small amounts of sugar (less than 2.5 g glucose per 100 ml of water) and electrolytes (less than 10 mEq sodium and 5 mEq potassium per liter of solution). (5,6)

4. Runners should be encouraged to frequently ingest fluids during competition and to consume 400–500 ml (13–17 oz.) of fluid 10–15 minutes before competition. (5,6,9)

5. Rules prohibiting the administration of fluids during the first 10 kilometers (6.2 miles) of a marathon race should be amended to permit fluid ingestion at frequent intervals along the race course. In light of the

*Adapted from Minard, D. *Prevention of heat casualties in Marine Corps Recruits.* *Milit. Med.* 126:261, 1961. WB-GT = 0.7 (WBT) + 0.2 (GT) + 0.1 (DBT)

high sweat rates and body temperatures during distance running in the heat, race sponsors should provide "water stations" at 3–4 kilometer (2–2.5 mile) intervals for all races of 16 kilometers (10 miles) or more. (4,8,9)

6. Runners should be instructed in how to recognize the early warning symptoms that precede heat injury. Recognition of symptoms, cessation of running, and proper treatment can prevent heat injury. Early warning symptoms include the following: piloerection on chest and upper arms, chilling, throbbing pressure in the head, unsteadiness, nausea, and dry skin. (2,9)

7. Race sponsors should make prior arrangements with medical personnel for the care of cases of heat injury. Responsible and informed personnel should supervise each "feeding station." Organizational personnel should reserve the right to stop runners who exhibit clear signs of heat stroke or heat exhaustion.

It is the position of the American College of Sports Medicine that policies established by local, national, and international sponsors of distance running events should adhere to these guidelines. Failure to adhere to these guidelines may jeopardize the health of competitors through heat injury.

appendix f

NUTRITION RECOMMENDATIONS FOR OARSWOMEN

Diet records, skin-fat-fold evaluations, and blood tests of candidates for our University's women's crew, have all helped identify certain nutrition-related problems which can be expected to compromise performance. Each of them could be easily corrected. The following suggestions may be helpful in conditioning for competition.

Adequate Diets

A good diet can be eaten in a traditional three-meals-a-day pattern, or with any number of divergent eating styles. The common practice of eating snacks and one meal a day can provide good nutrition, if all of the foods are thoughtfully selected. The first essential of any good diet is choosing a wide diversity of foods; and the Basic Diet (Chapter 2), which utilizes the guideline of the Four Food Groups, provides an appropriately varied diet.

The Basic Diet generally provides all nutrient needs, but it will have to be calorically supplemented to meet the energy needs of rowing. Larger than average servings and second servings will provide some additional calories. Even high-calorie preferences—like chocolate cream pie!—can be added in proportion to energy expenditure and caloric needs.

In some instances iron demands may not be met by the Basic Diet, and any oarswoman found to be anemic or iron depleted will need a medicinal iron supplement. A cautionary word: all female athletes using intrauterine devices should have their iron status checked with a blood test.

Weight and Fatness Control

The optimum level of fatness for women athletes has not yet been established. Studies of women distance runners and certain other endurance competitors suggest that degrees of fatness associated with top performance by women are not different than those for men: 5 to 7 per cent of total body weight. Recent estimates of body fatness of 46 oarswomen at the University of Washington revealed only five to have less than 10 per cent body fat. This is not an unusual ratio, and most oarswomen should reduce their level of fatness to be more fit and to improve their rowing performance. Others may want to reduce body weight to qualify for competition with the light-weight crew.

Considerations of Energy Balance in Reducing Body Fat

Excess body fat is stored energy. It can be reduced only when energy expenditure is greater than the intake of food energy. One gram of fat has an energy equivalent of 9 Calories. A pound of body fat represents roughly 3500 Calories of fat, somewhat more than the total amount of energy an oarswoman in active training will probably expend in an entire day. Thus, if the oarswoman is normally active and eats absolutely nothing for an entire day (a very bad practice), she will lose less than one pound of fat. Jogging for an hour may result in the expenditure of 500–700 Calories; at these rates, seven hours of jogging would result in the loss of 1½ pounds of fat. But rapid losses of weight, such as two pounds or more a day, represent losses of body water and not reduction of body fatness. Even total starvation will result in only gradual loss of weight. In fact, total starvation results in approximately equal losses of protein and fat tissue—obviously, an undesirable pattern.

How to Reduce Body Fat

The basis for any reducing program is creating a negative energy balance (i.e., expending more energy than is taken in); the following program is based on a modest increase in daily energy expenditure and a modest decrease in daily food intake. The increase in exercise must be realistic in its demands and compatible with academic and social commitments. An increased energy expenditure of approximately 500 Calories a day is usually recommended. This can be accomplished by 40 to 60 minutes of running, cycling, "stair-climbing," or swimming.

The diet reduction of 500 Calories is advised in conjunction with an intake of no less than 1600 or 1800 Calories. Lower energy intakes will result in more rapid weight loss, but in losses of muscle as well as fat; and energy intake will not be adequate to sustain daily academic activities, an even temperament, or good competitive performance.

Reducing food intake by 500 Calories and increasing energy expenditure by 500 Calories will create a 1000-Calorie energy deficit each day—a 7000-Calorie deficit each week, the equivalent of two pounds of body fat. This moderate weight reduction schedule is compatible with maintaining normal activity and eating patterns.

Two sample Basic Diet menus, supplying a daily intake of 1800 Calories, are given below. Smaller individuals may reduce this diet to 1600 Calories by lowering the margarine and oil intake and eliminating one of the roll, muffin, or bread servings. As stated previously, the food can be eaten at any time of the day (or night); the timing has no effect on fat loss. It's the total energy intake and expenditure that counts.

SAMPLE MENU #1

Breakfast

   Chilled half grapefruit
¾ cup dry cereal
1 cup skim milk
1 soft-cooked egg (optional)
1 slice toast
1 teaspoon special margarine
1 teaspoon marmalade
2 teaspoons sugar for cereal,
    fruit, or beverage
   Coffee or tea

Lunch

   Tomato stuffed with
    chicken salad (use 1
    tomato; ½ cup diced
    chicken; 2 tablespoons
    mayonnaise; capers;
    parsley; celery; lettuce)
1 large or 2 small hard rolls
1 teaspoon special margarine
1 cup skim milk
1 small banana, sliced
   Coffee or tea

Dinner

   Baked fish fillet (4 oz.)
    (use 1 teaspoon oil and
    ¼ cup bread crumbs)
   Broccoli with 1½
    teaspoons Hollandaise
    sauce
   Scalloped tomatoes (use ½
    cup canned tomatoes; 1
    slice diced bread; 1
    teaspoon oil; salt;
    pepper; basil)
1 slice Boston brown bread
1 teaspoon special margarine
1 canned pear, sweetened
    with syrup
   Coffee or tea

SAMPLE MENU #2

Breakfast

½   cup orange juice
2   plain muffins
1   teaspoon special margarine
1   cup skim milk
    Coffee or tea

Lunch

    Roast beef sandwich (use
        2 thin slices-3 oz. lean
        roast beef; 2 slices
        bread)
½   cup cole slaw with 1
        tablespoon mayonnaise
    Sliced sour pickles
1   cup skim milk
    Coffee or tea

Dinner

½   cup chilled fruit juice
¼   barbecued chicken (3 oz.)
        with 2 teaspoons oil
2   small ears corn, or 1 large
        ear, with 2 teaspoons
        special margarine
½   cup mixed carrots and peas
    Mixed green salad
1   tablespoon French dressing
1   slice French bread
½   cup sherbet
    Coffee or tea

There may not be enough time to "make weight" by losing at a rate of two pounds per week. The necessary rate of weight loss can be easily calculated and the total negative caloric expenditure estimated (at 3500 Calories per pound). *No one should attempt to lose more than 4 lbs./week.* Thus, it's essential to "plan ahead."

If it is necessary to increase the rate of weight loss to three-to-four pounds a week, the necessary increase in negative caloric balance should come from *increasing exercise*—not from a further reduction of food intake. An additional hour of vigorous exercise each day will reduce body fat slightly more than a pound a week. Don't eat less than 1600 Calories a day.

appendix g

PARTICIPATION IN SPORTS BY GIRLS

Until recently, girls and women have been deprived of their rightful share in physical recreation and sports by traditional concepts about a socially acceptable feminine image, misconceptions about the extent to which females may safely participate in strenuous activity, and, in fact, society's whole previous notion about woman's role and her basic needs and her physical capabilities.

Customary safeguards for protection of health and safety of males in sports and competitive athletics should apply to girls and women. Thus, competent medical care before, during, and after participation, rigorous conditioning, suitable high-quality equipment, good playing facilities, competent coaching, and capable officiating are necessary for the safety of all who engage in sports and competitive athletics.

To assist physicians who may be involved in making decisions regarding participation in sports by girls and young women, the Committee offers the following guidelines:

1. There is no reason to separate prepubescent children by sex in sports, physical education, and recreational activities.

2. Girls can compete against girls in any sports activity if matched for size, weight, skill, and physical maturation as long as the safeguards mentioned above are followed.

3. Girls can attain high levels of physical fitness through strenuous conditioning activities to improve their physical fitness, agility, strength, appearance, endur-

ance, and sense of psychic well-being. These have no
unfavorable influence on menstruation, future pregnancy, and childbirth.[1]

4. Postpubescent girls should not participate against boys
   in heavy collision sports because of the grave risk of
   serious injury due to their lesser muscle mass per unit
   of body weight.

5. The talented female athlete may participate on a team
   with boys in an appropriate sport provided that the
   school or community offers opportunities for all girls
   to participate in comparable activities.

The best interests of girls and women in sports activities
are served by opportunities to experience the thrill of sports
competition when they are able to qualify for girls' programs
sponsored just for them. Ultimate benefits are greater when
efforts are directed to developing girls' programs and the
athletes within them, rather than emphasizing the exceptional
female athlete who may wish to participate with boys on their
teams.

COMMITTEE ON PEDIATRIC ASPECTS OF PHYSICAL FITNESS,
RECREATION, AND SPORTS

MELVIN L. THORNTON, M.D., *Chairman*
GLORIA D. ENG, M.D.
JOHN H. KENNELL, M.D.
ROBERT N. McLEOD, JR., M.D.
THOMAS E. SHAFFER, M.D.

[1]Corbitt, R. W., Cooper, D. L., Erickson, D. J., Kriss, F. C., Thornton, M. L., and Craig, T. T.: Female athletics. JAMA, 228:1266, 1974.

Index*

Adenosine triphosphate, 75–79
Aerobic metabolism, 75
Air Travel, 92
Alcohol, 59
Aldosterone, 96
Amino acids, 13,16
Anabolic agents, 64
Anaerobic metabolism, 75
Androgen hormones, 63, 64, 158
Anemia, 9
Ascorbic acid, 9
Atherosclerosis, 11
Atkins, Dr.–"Diet Revolution", 44
ATP, 75–79

Basic Seven Plan, 28
Beriberi, 8
Biotin, 6, 9
Body fat, 135

Caffeine, 120
Calcium, 4, 18, 29, 95
Calorimeter, 57
Cal-power®, 81, 83
Carbon, 12
Carbon dioxide, 12
Cardiovascular disease, 11
Cathartics, 141
Cellulose, 15
Cholesterol, 10
Cobalamin, 9
Convulsions, 9

Dianabol, 63, 149
Diuretics, 141

Electrolytes, 92
Ensure®, 120
Essential amino acids, 17
Estrogen, 64
Extracellular fluids, 4, 91, 94, 95

Fat-soluble vitamins, 8, 10, 45
Ferritin, 107
Fluorides, 19
Fluorine, 4
Folic acid, 7, 9, 30
Four Food Groups, 28–32, 68, 156
Fruitarian Diet, 42

Glucose, 12, 14, 15
Glycogen, 13, 76, 80, 81
Goiter, 5

Health foods, 43
Hemoglobin, 107, 108
Hemoglobin formation, 18
"High Energol" capsules, 45
High-salt foods, 133
Hy-Cal®, 83
Hydrogen, 12

*The more general references, apparent in the Table of Contents, have been omitted.

Insensible water loss, 92
Instant breakfasts, 86
Intracellular fluid, 95
Involuntary hypohydration, 94
Iodine, 4, 5, 19
Iron, Chap. 7, p. 5, 18

Jet-lag, 92
Jet flight, 124

Kilo-calorie, 52

Lactase, 12
Lactose, 12
Lacto-vegetarian diet, 19, 36–42
Linoleic acid, 10

Magnesium, 4, 95
Metabolic water, 92
Metallic ions, 4, 95
Multi-vitamin capsules, 45

Niacin, 8
Nutritional supplements, 141

Organic foods, 43
Osmotic pressure, 96
Oxygen, 12

Pantothenic acid, 6, 9
"PC", 76
Pellagra, 8
Pernicious anemia, 9
Phosphocreatine, 76
Phosphorous, 4
Poly-cose®, 81
Potassium, 4, 95, 141
Potassium salts, 98
Powdered milk, 29
Protein supplements, 48

Provitamin A, 8
Pyridoxine, 9

Riboflavin, 29
Rickets, 6

Saturated fat, 11
Scurvy, 6, 9
Skin-fold,
    measurements, App. D
    composition, 65, 66, 135
Sodium, 4, 95
Sucrose, 12, 15
"Super 96 Protein", 48, 49
Sustacal®, 120
Sustagen®, 120

Ten-state Survey, 110
Testosterone, 63
Thiamine, 7
Thyroxin, 5, 19
Tryglycerides, 10

Unsaturated fat, 11
Urea, 16

Vitamin A, 6, 18
Vitamin B-complex, 6
Vitamin B_{12}, 9, 42
Vitamin C, 6, 30, 46, 47
Vitamin D, 6, 18
Vitamin E, 6, 18, 46, 47
Vitamin K, 6, 18

"Water pills", 131, 144
"Who's Who in American Sports", 153

Xerophthalmia, 8

Zen Macrobiotic Diet, 42
Zinc, 5, 19